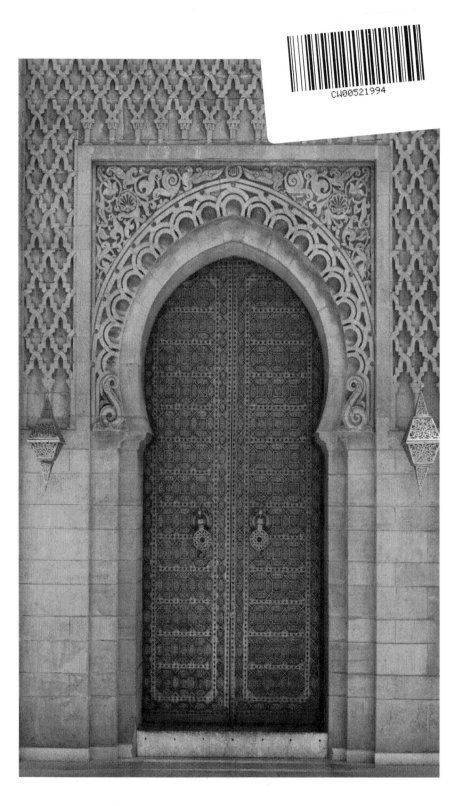

Morocco Travel Guide

Discover the Most Captivating Itineraries from Marrakech Medina to Chefchaouen's Cobalt Alleyways | Expert Tips & Hidden Gems for Your Seamless Arabian Adventure

RACHID ALAOUI

Table of Contents

CHAPTER FOUR 10 EXCITING OUTDOOR ADVENTURES TO EXPERIENCE 71

CHAPTER FIVE TRAVEL PLANS 75

CHAPTER SIX TOP ACCOMMODATION OPTIONS IN MOROCCO 91

INTRODUCTION

Morocco, a country in North Africa, is often regarded as one of the most visually stunning locations on the planet. The remains of its long-ago history mingle with the characteristics of its modern self. Morocco is also one of the most diverse countries in the world since it has enormous mountains, a vast desert, a breathtaking coastline, and valleys that are filled with trees. This beautiful nation can meet the needs of each traveler since it has hundreds of old walled cities, unspoiled sand beaches, and lively open-air markets. Morocco has significant historical importance because of the remarkable geographical position it occupies and the agricultural resources it has. Geographically speaking, the country of Morocco may be found in the Maghreb region of North Africa. It is a sizeable country with a population of over 33.8 million people and an area of 446,550 km2, respectively. Rabat is the official capital of Morocco, although Casablanca is the most populous city in the country.

The country of Morocco, also known officially as the Kingdom of Morocco, is home to an incredible diversity of gorgeous places that are just waiting to be discovered. On your route from the massive capital city of Rabat to the Atlantic Coast and Casablanca, you will be able to pass through some of the most breathtaking landscapes on the face of the planet. The stunning natural scenery of Morocco never fails to astonish visitors. There is a significant amount of Spanish influence in the architecture of Morocco, particularly in the monuments and structures that have been preserved. This architecture can be seen all around the country. The narrow alleyways and streets lined with cobblestone may include trendy boutiques as well as cutting-edge restaurants and cafés. The most significant source of revenue for Morocco is tourism, which draws visitors from all over the globe to the country's kilometers of coastline, old medinas, and a plethora of natural beauties. The country also has a large labor force, which contributes to the country's high standard of living.

You should go to Morocco if you want to unwind, take a holiday, or enjoy a long weekend away from the hustle and bustle of everyday life. Away from the bustle of everyday life, quiet walkways and seemingly infinite trails wind through wildlife that has not been touched by human hands. However, the nation as a whole provides a wide variety of opportunities to spend one's time and experience something entirely new. This is made possible by the many hospitable cities and charming villages that dot the landscape. Those who prefer a more contemporary way of life may choose from a wide variety of activities, like tourism and shopping, while they are here. The country is divided into twelve areas, each of which is distinguished by its natural splendor, spectacular architecture, and thriving culture. Every region has its personality, appeal, scenery, and even food to offer visitors and residents alike. Because of its extensive coastline, diverse geology, and temperature, Morocco is home to a plethora of great towns, villages, and spots to discover. Each city has at least one aspect that is just breathtaking.

CHAPTER ONE
WHAT YOU NEED FOR A TRIP TO MOROCCO

WHAT ITEMS SHOULD BE CARRIED ALONG?

In preparing your luggage for a vacation to Morocco, it is vital to take into consideration the weather, the activities you want to participate in, and the cultural standards of the country. To assist you in packing for your vacation, the following is a basic packing guide:

ITEM 1: Necessary Traveling Items

1. Passport/Visa:

You should always have your passport, visa, and any other needed identification or travel papers with you at all times.

2. Moroccan Dirhams, Credit/Debit Cards:

If you plan on making larger purchases while in Morocco, bring either a credit card or a debit card in addition to some Moroccan dirhams for smaller transactions.

3. *Power adapter:*

Electrical outlets in Morocco are generally of the Type C and Type E kind; thus, if your electronic devices use a different type of plug, you will need to bring along the proper power adapter.

4. *Basic Medications:*

When packing your first aid kit, be sure to include basic medications, bandages, and any personal medicines that you may need while you are away from home.

5. *Travel insurance:*

Purchasing travel insurance that protects you against unexpected occurrences, such as the need for emergency medical care and trip cancellations, is a sound investment at all times.

ITEM 2: Clothing

Pack light, loose-fitting clothing made of natural fabrics such as cotton or linen that are breathable since it may become rather warm in Morocco, particularly in the summertime.

Show proper courtesy to the people of the region by dressing modestly, particularly if you plan on traveling to more rural areas or religious sites. Shoulder protection is essential for women; therefore, they should always have a scarf or shawl on hand to use as needed.

Bring a light jacket or sweater with you since evenings may turn cold, particularly in locations with a desert or mountainous terrain, and it is a smart idea to do so.

When traveling through Morocco's cities, it is a good idea to bring along a pair of shoes that are not only comfortable but also suitable for long walks over rugged terrain.

ITEM 3: Objects connected with the weather

Carry weather-related items like:

1. Sun Protection
2. Rain Gear

1. Sun Protection:

Sun protection is required in the form of a hat, sunscreen, and sunglasses in Morocco since the sun can be rather intense there.

2. Rain Gear:

Bring an umbrella and a waterproof coat if you plan on traveling between November through February. This is the rainy season in this region, so be prepared for wet weather.

ITEM 4: Additional items

1. Toiletries:

Be sure you include all of your essential amenities, including shampoo, soap, a toothbrush, and toothpaste, in a travel size. Wet wipes and hand sanitizer are two other helpful items.

2. Electronics:

Don't forget to bring your phone, camera, and any necessary charging cables. A travel adapter that works for a variety of devices might be useful.

3. Backpack:

A tiny backpack or daypack is useful for bringing supplies while traveling on day excursions or visiting new locations. This is because a backpack may be worn on its back.

4. *Water container:*

To avoid producing unnecessary waste and to ensure that you always have access to water, always have a refillable water bottle on you. This will help you stay hydrated.

THE TIME OF YEAR THAT IS MOST FAVORABLE FOR A VISIT

The preferences and interests of the visitor, in addition to the locations in Morocco that they want to visit, will determine the best time for them to go to Morocco. The diverse topography of Morocco, which stretches from the coast to the mountains to the desert, is the root reason for the country's wide range of climates.

The following is a rundown of the many seasons and the relative appeal of traveling during each one:

Spring (March-May)

Many people say that the springtime in Morocco, namely the months of March through May, is the best time to visit the country. The temperature is just right, the flowers are blooming, and it's a beautiful day to be outdoors. The weather is beautiful, and it is the ideal time to go sightseeing and discover new cities like Casablanca, Fes, and Marrakech.

Summer (June -August)

The summers in Morocco may become quite hot, especially in the interior and in the Sahara Desert. Essaouira and Agadir are two seaside cities in Morocco that have a more temperate climate. You may still have a nice time in Morocco at this time of year, provided that you can tolerate the heat. The cooler temperatures and the many opportunities for hiking that the Atlas Mountains provide are a welcome break.

Autumn (September-November)

If you are interested in experiencing Moroccan culture, another wonderful season to come to Morocco is during the autumn months (September to November). Temperatures are more bearable than they were during the warm summer months, and the sun is shining brightly. Both the well-known Agadir Timitar Festival and the M'Hamid El Ghizlane International Nomad Festival take place at this time of year.

Winter (December-February)

During the winter months (December to February), Morocco has colder temperatures, notably at night in the desert and highlands. Coastal regions, on the other hand, continue to have a moderate climate. The Atlas Mountains are a great place to go skiing and other winter activities because of their terrain. In addition, the Sahara Desert is at its prime for exploration during this time of year since the temperatures throughout the middle of the day are more tolerable.

ARRIVING THERE AND NAVIGATING YOUR SURROUNDINGS

You may go to Morocco and get about the country in several different ways thanks to the availability of various possibilities.

The following is an overview of how to go to Morocco as well as how to move about once you are there:

Through Land:

If you are currently in a country that is near Morocco, you may want to consider entering Morocco through land. There are shared boundaries between Morocco and the Western Sahara. There are several land border crossings; however, before taking this route, be careful to clarify whether or not a visa is required, as well as whether or not there are any travel warnings.

Moving By Air:

Flying to Morocco is the fastest and most comfortable method to get there. The country's three principal international airports are located at Casablanca's Mohammed V International Airport, Marrakech's Menara Airport, and Agadir (Agadir Al Massira Airport). Mohammed V International Airport is located in Casablanca. These airports serve as landing spots for flights coming from significant cities located all over the globe. When you are there, you will have access to a variety of forms of transportation, including domestic planes as well as other options, which will allow you to travel across the country.

Visa

You may need a visa to enter Morocco if your country of citizenship is not one of the countries that Morocco recognizes as visa-exempt. Contact the Moroccan embassy or consulate in your country to inquire about the requirements for obtaining a visa and the specific terms and circumstances of your trip.

TRANSIT INSIDE MOROCCO

Once you are in Morocco, you have several alternatives for getting to different parts of the nation, including:

Using Trains:

Morocco's large rail infrastructure links its major cities and facilitates travel across the country. Trains are a well-liked mode of transportation for long-distance journeys because they are comfortable, trustworthy, and convenient.

Using Taxis:

Two distinct types of taxis may be found in urban areas, and they are referred to as petit taxis and grand taxis, respectively. Petit taxis are smaller, more compact taxis that operate just inside the boundaries of a city, while grand taxis are larger, more spacious taxis that travel between cities or to rural regions. When taking a ride in a tiny cab, it is very necessary to negotiate the cost or demand that the driver use the meter.

Using Car Rental:

When you hire a car, you not only have the ability to go to far-off destinations but also the flexibility to do so. You may pick up a rental vehicle at any of Morocco's airports or in any of the country's cities, where you'll find the presence of some well-known car rental firms. However, you should always be prepared for a variety of driving conditions, regulations of the road, and manners when you are on the road.

Using Buses:

Buses are yet another prevalent kind of transportation that operates in both urban and rural settings. Bus services connecting many different cities are provided by private operators and corporations such as CTM and Supratours.

Using Shared Transportation:

When traveling between cities, locals typically use minivans that are shared by many passengers. These vehicles are also sometimes referred to as "big taxis" or "supra tours." These options may be more cost-effective than others, but they do not adhere to regular schedules.

COMMUNICATION AND THE USE OF LANGUAGE

The people of Morocco speak both Arabic and French, making it a fully multilingual country. In all administrative and professional settings, Moroccans communicate in Modern Standard Arabic since it is the country's official language. In addition to Arabic, Moroccans are fluent in some other languages as well.

The following are some of the reasons why language and communication are so essential in Morocco:

Importance of Language and Communication in Morocco

The Morocco Darija

The Moroccan Arabic language, which is more often referred to as Darija, is the language that is spoken the most in Morocco. It is a form of Arabic that has major deviations from the Modern Standard form of the language. The various loanwords from Berber, French, and Spanish languages that can be found in Darija serve to illustrate the historical and cultural influences that have had an impact on Morocco. Daily life in Morocco is mostly conducted in Darija, the national language.

Languages Spoken by the Berber Community

The Berber community accounts for a considerable portion of Morocco's population, and its members speak their own distinct set of languages. Both Tamazight and Tarifit are examples of Berber languages that are widely used in Morocco. Tamazight is the most widely spoken. These languages, each of which has its unique dialect, are frequently spoken in rural areas and in communities that are located in more remote areas.

English

The younger generation of Moroccans, in particular, has shown a marked improvement in their command of the English language. English is a subject that is studied in both secondary and tertiary education settings due to its pervasive use in the tourist industry and international business environments.

French

Because of its history as a French colony, Morocco has a substantial number of people who speak French. It continues to be an important language in many spheres, including education, media, business, and government. Because of this, French is commonly used as a language of difference and social standing in Morocco, and a significant number of Moroccans are fluent in both Arabic and French.

Spanish

As a result of historical ties and the geographical closeness of Morocco to Spain, several Moroccans are fluent in Spanish. This is especially true in the northern region of Morocco, in cities such as Tangier and Tetouan. In addition, several institutions provide teaching in Spanish, which, depending on the circumstances, might be beneficial to one's ability to communicate.

In their interpersonal interactions, Moroccans often place a higher value on indirectness, civility, and hospitality than other forms of direct communication. People often exchange pleasantries and engage in small chat with one another at the outset of a conversation before moving on to the primary subject of discussion. When it comes to nonverbal communication, making use of gestures and facial expressions is quite important for both developing rapport and conveying messages.

NOTE: It is essential to keep in mind that a person's level of language proficiency and usage might vary greatly based on their degree of education, their upbringing, and the region of Morocco in which they were raised. The variety of languages spoken in Morocco, on the other hand, contributes to the country's rich cultural heritage and makes it a fascinating location for the study of linguistics.

LANGUAGE BASICS YOU SHOULD KNOW BEFORE TRAVELING TO MOROCCO

To improve your ability to communicate with locals and have a deeper understanding of the culture, it is recommended that you study some basic phrases in a foreign language before traveling to Morocco. The following are a few essential phrases in Arabic and French, although both languages enjoy widespread usage:

ARABIC (DARIJA):

WORDS	MEANING
Salaam alaikum	"Hello." (also means "Peace be upon you."
Shukran	"Thank you"
Afak (which you should pronounce "a-fak")	"Please"
Laa	"no"
Naam	"yes"
Kayfa haluk?	"How are you doing?"
Min fadlak (used to catch someone's attention)	Excuse me
Biddi wahed	I would like one of (used to express that you would want one of something)
Hal tatakallamou al-Ingliziya?	Do you speak English?
Ma'a Salama	"With peace"

FRENCH

WORDS	MEANING
Bonjour	Hello
Merci	Thank you
S'il vous plaît	Please
Non	No
Oui	Yes
Comment ça va?	How are you?
Excusez-moi	Excuse me (to get someone's attention)
Je voudrais un/une...	I would like a...
Parlez-vous anglais?	Do you speak English?
Au revoir	Goodbye

Your ability to exhibit respect for the culture of the community and to improve your relationships with Moroccans may be enhanced by learning and using the following phrases. Even in more remote locations or among older generations, it is essential to keep in mind that not everyone you meet will comprehend these languages. This is true even if they were born in the country. Being patient, having an open mind, and being ready to utilize basic English as well as gestures are all important components in the process of overcoming language barriers.

MONEY AND FINANCIAL INSTITUTIONS

The official currency of the nation of Morocco is known as the dirham. The currency code for the dirham is MAD. The following information on banking and the local currency is given for the convenience of tourists:

Currency that is Accepted

The Moroccan dirham is the country's official currency; however, many tourist spots, hotels, and larger organizations also take the euro and the United States dollar as payment. It is recommended that you have some cash on hand at all times for use with local merchants, taxis, and neighborhood markets.

Currency Conversion

It is recommended that you exchange your money for Moroccan dirhams as soon as possible after arriving in Morocco. You may complete this task at international airports, bureaux de change, authorized currency exchange merchants, and banks. It is in your best interest to examine different exchange rates and prices to get the best deal.

Automated teller Machines

In Moroccan cities and towns, there is widespread availability of ATMs, and these machines accept most major credit and debit cards issued internationally, including Visa and Mastercard. You may receive Moroccan dirhams from ATMs if you use your card to make the transaction. It is always a good idea to inform your bank of your travel plans to ensure that your credit card will continue to work properly while you are away.

Credit Cards

Credit cards are often accepted in bigger establishments such as hotels, upscale restaurants, and stores. However, due to the possibility that certain smaller businesses and restaurants would not accept credit cards, it is recommended that you bring some cash with you or use a debit card.

Banks

The hours of operation for banks in Morocco are typically Monday through Friday, 8:30 a.m. to 4:30 p.m. Some banks may have shorter hours on Saturdays. Banks provide a wide variety of services, such as the ability to withdraw cash, convert money, and get assistance with traveler's checks.

Traveler's Checks

Traveler's checks are not often accepted in Morocco, and it may be challenging to locate establishments that will cash them. In most situations, it is preferable to combine the use of cash with credit cards for increased convenience.

NOTE: When you travel, it is very necessary to take precautions to prevent your money and your personal information from being stolen. Utilize automated teller machines that are situated in protected places, keep an eye on your belongings, and avoid drawing attention to large sums of cash that you are carrying.

ETIQUETTE AND OTHER CULTURAL NORMS

Morocco is a nation with a cultural history that is both extensive and varied.

The following is some information on the culture of Morocco for tourists:

1. Hospitality

Hospitality in Morocco Moroccans are well recognized for their warm and welcoming nature. Visitors are regularly welcomed into the homes of locals for a cup of tea or a whole supper. Accepting such invitations is a fantastic opportunity to get insight into the culture of Morocco as well as the manner of life that is prevalent in the region.

2. The cuisine of Morocco

The cuisine of Morocco is well-known for its robust tastes and aromatic spices. Traditional dishes include couscous, tagines (a kind of stew cooked over low heat for many hours), and pastilla, which is a savory pastry stuffed with meat and spices. In Morocco, mint tea is a well-liked beverage that is usually served as a gesture of hospitality and friendship. Do not be afraid to taste local delicacies such as "pastilla" and "msemen," which are both types of bread that are pan-fried, as well as grilled meats (a savory pie).

3. Courtesy and Politeness

The Moroccans put a great value on hospitality, and greetings play an important part in their way of life. Etiquette and pleasantries are also very important in Morocco. The customary method of greeting someone is to give them a handshake while using the Arabic phrase "Salaam alaikum," which translates to "peace be upon you." Men may also kiss one another on the cheek when they get together with close friends or family. This often occurs during social gatherings. At all times and in all circumstances, but particularly when one is in a religious environment, respect and humility should be demonstrated.

4. Attire

Regardless of Morocco's typically liberal society, it is advisable to dress modestly, particularly in rural or traditional regions. Dressing in a manner characteristic of the West is generally acceptable in more tourist-oriented cities like Casablanca and Marrakech; nevertheless, it is recommended that visitors wear clothing that is more modest while visiting mosques or other places of religious worship. Women should consider carrying a scarf with them at all times if they are required to cover their heads.

5. Traditional Arts and Crafts

Morocco is well-known for its traditional arts and crafts. You may discover beautiful mosaic tilework, brass lanterns, colorful pottery, and gorgeous hand-woven carpets in the souks, which are the local marketplaces. Haggling is a common practice in Moroccan marketplaces, so there is no need to be afraid to do it. Islamic Culture Islam is the dominant religion in this nation, and its influence may be seen in many aspects of everyday life. Visitors are expected to demonstrate respect for Islamic traditions as well as sensitivity to local cultures. During the holy month of Ramadan, when Muslims fast from dawn to sunset, it is considered courteous to refrain from eating, drinking, or smoking in public.

6. Celebrations and Festivity

Throughout the year, Morocco commemorates a variety of religious and cultural festivals. The most important holiday is Eid al-Fitr, which marks the end of Ramadan and is celebrated with eating, getting together with extended family, and giving gifts. The Mawazine World Rhythms Festival in Rabat, the Gnaoua World Music Festival in Essaouira, and the Marrakech International Film Festival are some of the other events that will be taking place.

THE CUSTOM OF GIVING IN MOROCCO

Tipping, also known as "baksheesh," is a common practice that is acknowledged and appreciated by the people receiving one's services. It is customary to leave a tip as a sign of gratitude for exceptional service, even though doing so is not obligatory. When it comes to tipping, here are some things to keep in mind:

Hotels

It is customary to leave gratuities for the hotel staff, particularly the porters who assist you with your luggage. You may leave between 10 and 20 dirhams as a gratuity for each bag. It is also common practice to provide the employees who clean the rooms a tip of a few dollars each day.

Cafés and Bars

Although tipping is not customary in cafés and bars, you may still express your gratitude to the staff by leaving some extra change or by rounding the total up to the next dollar.

Tour Guides and Drivers

It is customary to tip them if you have a tour guide or driver for a lengthier tour or a day trip. This is also the case if you have a tour guide or driver for a day trip. The price of the service may increase or decrease according to factors such as the length of time it is performed and its overall quality. As a matter of thumb, you should plan on tipping your tour guide and driver between 50 and 100 dirhams for each day of their services.

Restaurants

In restaurants, it is customary to leave a tip that is equivalent to roughly 10 percent of the whole cost. Check the whole amount of the bill to ensure that it does not contain any hidden or additional service charges before giving a tip. If you felt that the service was exceptional, you are free to leave a more generous tip.

Additional Activities

It is common to leave a tip at other facilities, such as hair salons, spas, and hammams (traditional Turkish baths), among other places. You are welcome to leave a tip of up to 10 percent of the total service charge if you are satisfied with the work that was done for you.

CHAPTER TWO
BENEFITS OF TAKING A TRIP TO MOROCCO

Morocco is an enthralling country that has a rich history, a diverse range of landscapes, and vibrant cultural traditions.

The following is a list of ten compelling reasons you should consider a trip to Morocco:

1. Lively and Unique Culture

The culture of Morocco is distinctive and vibrant because it is the product of a complex confluence of influences from Arabs, Berbers, and Europeans. The country of Morocco is home to a variety of cultural riches that are open for exploration. These treasures include the lively medinas and ancient monuments, such as the old city of Marrakech, as well as the well-preserved Roman ruins of Volubilis.

2. Commands Attractive and Stunning Architecture

The country is also well-known for its stunning architecture, which is characterized by intricate geometric shapes, vivid colors, and excellent tilework. The magnificent design of

Morocco's architecture may be seen in the country's well-known mosques, palaces, and riads, which are the country's traditional houses.

3. The Country has Many Stunning Cities

Morocco is home to many stunning cities that are a delight to discover and are among the country's top tourist attractions. Because of its pulsating souks, lively Djemaa el-Fna square, and gorgeous palaces, Marrakech is an absolute must-see trip. Other cities, like Fes, Casablanca, and Chefchaouen, each have their special allure to offer visitors.

4. It Has the Sahara Desert as One of its Natural Beauties

The Sahara Desert is perhaps one of the most breathtaking natural wonders that Morocco has to offer. When you go on an excursion across the desert, you will have the opportunity to enjoy camel riding, gaze at the stars under the clear desert sky, and experience the traditional hospitality of the Berber people who live in the desert camps.

5. It Possesses Magnificent Mountains

The Atlas Mountains provide a dramatic backdrop for the country of Morocco's surroundings. It doesn't matter whether you're hiking in the majestic High Atlas Mountains, discovering the beautiful Ourika Valley, or traveling to the mountain towns of the Rif Mountains: the many mountain ranges of the country provide spectacular vistas and exciting opportunities for outdoor recreation.

6. Diverse Range of Landscapes

Morocco has a diverse range of landscapes, ranging from the Sahara Desert to the beaches of the Mediterranean and Atlantic oceans. You may go from lounging on gorgeous beaches to exploring green valleys and wandering through a rich oasis in a short period. This is all possible because of the region's diverse topography.

7. Aromatic and Savory Cuisine

The cuisine of Morocco is famous for its aromatic and savory meals, which come in a wide variety. Do not miss the opportunity to taste traditional Moroccan cuisine, such as tagines, couscous, aromatic mint tea, and exquisite sweets such as baklava. There is a wide range of delectable cuisines and gastronomical experiences to be had in the nation's food markets and street sellers.

8. Friendly and Warm Hospitality

Moroccans are known for their outgoing personalities and their warm hospitality. You may expect to find yourself regularly surrounded by hospitable individuals who will invite you to have a meal or a cup of tea and who will immerse you in the distinctive cultural practices of the country.

9. Historical Ancient Medinad

A trip to one of Morocco's cities' medinas, often known as "ancient city sections," is like taking a trip back in time. Spend some time wandering around the meandering lanes that resemble a labyrinth and are dotted with shops offering handcrafted products, textiles, and spices. In particular, the medinas of Fes and Marrakech, both of which are included on the list of UNESCO World Heritage Sites, provide a glimpse into Morocco's ancient past.

10. Lively and Exciting Festivity

Throughout the year, Morocco plays home to a diverse range of exciting festivals and other types of events. These events provide you the opportunity to get completely submerged in the creative and cultural customs of the nation. From the pulsating spectacle of the Fes Festival of World Sacred Music to the energizing ambiance of the Marrakech International Film Festival, you will have the chance to experience everything that this country has to offer artistically and culturally.

CHAPTER THREE
PLACES OF INTEREST FOR TOURISTS IN MOROCCO

1. MARRAKECH

Marrakech is a city in Morocco that is known for its long history, gorgeous architecture, bustling marketplaces, and a mix of cultural influences. It is a lively and enticing city that is located in Morocco.

Let's take a look at some of the well-known tourist destinations, breathtaking parks, and hidden treasures that make Marrakech such an appealing destination.

A. Tourist Attractions:

Jemaa el-Fnaa:

Jemaa el-Fnaa, often known as the "old city," is a lively plaza that serves as the nerve center of Marrakech's medina. It is a UNESCO World Heritage site and a sensory feast, complete with food stalls, snake charmers, storytellers, musicians, and colorful street entertainment.

The Koutoubia Mosque:

The Koutoubia Mosque is a well-known landmark and the largest mosque in Marrakech. It has stunning architecture, and its minaret is quite remarkable.

The Bahia Palace:

The Bahia Palace is a superb example of Moroccan architecture, with spectacular courtyards, intricate tilework, and attractive gardens. It serves as the city's icon and is stunning from every vantage point. There is a peaceful oasis located right in the heart of the bustling city.

Majorelle Garden:

Jacques Majorelle, a French painter, was responsible for the creation of this botanical garden, which he intended to be a tranquil escape from the hectic city.

The Saadian Tombs:

The Saadian Tombs, which were discovered in 1917, provide a glimpse into the rich history of Marrakech. They are characterized by their peculiar flora, bright blue architecture, and a small museum dedicated to the culture of the Berber people.

One of the mausoleums, which is known for its magnificent decoration, serves as the last resting place for members of the Saadian dynasty.

B. Beaches and Parks:

Although Marrakech is an interior city and does not have beaches, there are choices for beach lovers within driving distance of the city.

Oualidia:

One of these possibilities is Oualidia, a hidden treasure with a beautiful lagoon and white sand beaches that is around three hours from Marrakech. Swimming, watching birds, and taking in the stunning vistas of the coastline are all wonderful things to do at this location.

C. Beautiful Parks:

Historic Menara Gardens:

The historic Menara Gardens are located close to the center of the city. These gardens have a huge reflecting lake with a background of the Atlas Mountains. Strolling, having a picnic, and just soaking in the serene ambiance of the area are common activities that people like doing here.

Agdal Gardens:

The Agdal Gardens are located close to the Royal Palace and include expansive green meadows, citrus groves, and lovely canals. Strolls in this serene haven are a favorite pastime for both locals and tourists alike.

D. Hidden Gems:

Exquisite Marrakech Garden:

The exquisite gardens of Marrakech, nestled away in the medina, give a calm getaway with lush vegetation, fountains, and unmarked walkways. These gardens may be found in the heart of the city.

Ancient Tanneries:

Although they are not exactly hidden, the ancient tanneries in the medina give an intriguing peek into the historical leather industry of Marrakech. It is the perfect location to go when you want to get away from the crowded streets and find some quiet. Visitors can see the dying and curing processes, although the smell may be excessive.

Yves Saint Laurent Museum:

The Yves Saint Laurent Museum was established to commemorate the world-famous fashion designer by demonstrating his creative output and love for Marrakech. In addition to hosting Moroccan fashion shows, it has a significant assortment of high-end couture goods.

REMEMBER: Marrakech is a city that provides each visitor with a one-of-a-kind and captivating experience by skillfully combining the city's rich history, vibrant culture, and stunning natural surroundings.

2. ESSAOUIRA

The lovely seaside city of Essaouira can be found on the Atlantic coast of Morocco, near the country's western edge. Essaouira is a popular destination for travelers who are looking for a blend of cultural experiences, opportunities for outdoor recreation, and natural beauty. It is known for its laid-back environment, historical importance, and stunning beaches.

A. Tourist Attractions:

Essaouira Medina:

The Medina of Essaouira, which is recognized on the UNESCO World Heritage List, is located in the center of the city and is a location that visitors just cannot miss. Explore the meandering alleyways decorated with whitewashed buildings and doors with beautiful blue trim, as well as the vibrant markets that are loaded with regional crafts, spices, and characteristic Moroccan items. In addition, discover the usual Moroccan goods.

Skala de la Ville:

Skala de la Ville has breathtaking views of both the city and the ocean, and it is located on top of a historic fort. It was intended to be a protective structure when it was built in the 18th century, but nowadays, people go there to watch the sunset.

Essaouira Ramparts:

The Medina is encompassed by well-preserved ramparts, which provide pleasant walks along the walls with expansive views of the city and the sea. The ramparts are a UNESCO World Heritage Site.

Mohammed Ben Abdallah Museum:

The Mohammed Ben Abdallah Museum is a museum that displays a broad variety of Moroccan artwork, such as paintings, jewelry, traditional attire, and historical relics. The museum is housed in a building that was once used as a palace.

Essaouira Beach:

With its large expanses of golden sand, Essaouira Beach is the perfect spot for swimming, windsurfing, and other sports that take place in water. Because of the beach's consistent wind patterns, it is popular with visitors from all over the globe.

B. Beaches and Parks:

Plage Tagharte:

Plage Tagharte is known for its lack of development. This pristine beach is approximately 20 minutes outside of Essaouira and is far less crowded than the most popular beach in the city. It is the ideal place for leisure activities and picnics since it is peaceful and has spectacular views, and it is situated south of Essaouira.

Sidi Kaouki Beach:

Sidi Kaouki Beach is a popular spot for surfers. The nearby dunes provide a picturesque background, and the combination of the powerful waves and the expansive sandy beach creates great conditions for surfing.

C. Hidden Gems:

Diabat Village:

Diabat is a little town located near Essaouira. It has a chill atmosphere and a laid-back atmosphere. It is commonly known that Jimi Hendrix and Cat Stevens were both affected by the village while they were developing their musical styles.

The Jewish Quarter:

The Jewish Quarter is a less well-known part of the Medina that gives an insight into Essaouira's multiethnic history. Visitors may enjoy a horseback ride along the beach, feel the rustic beauty of the neighborhood, and view the remnants of Jimi Hendrix's house. Visit the medieval synagogue, which is now a museum, and take a walk through the twisting passageways that are ornamented with blue doors.

Essaouira's Street Art:

Wander about the region and take in the flourishing street art culture in the city. By showcasing the talents of local, national, and even worldwide artists in the form of vivid murals and unique graffiti, Essaouira infuses its historically significant surroundings with a sense of contemporary vibrancy.

3. FES

The Moroccan city of Fes, more often known as Fez, is a thriving metropolis that is rich in amazing architecture, history, and culture. Fes is also the traditional capital of Morocco. It is one of the most intriguing areas in the country and provides a range of tourist attractions, magnificent beaches, parks, and unknown secrets. Additionally, it is one of the most beautiful spots in the country. Let's find out more about them:

A. Tourists Attractions:

Fes el-Bali:

Fes el-Bali is a UNESCO World Heritage site and the biggest and oldest medieval city in the world. It is also one of the most popular tourist destinations. This city offers visitors a glimpse into the traditional way of life in Morocco with its bustling souks, ancient mosques, and winding alleyways.

Al-Qarawiyyin Mosque:

The Al-Qarawiyyin Mosque and institution is considered to be the world's oldest continuously operating institution. The year 9000 marks the beginning of its existence. The mosque's library is one of the building's many architectural marvels that should not be missed.

Bou Inania Madrasa:

The Bou Inania Madrasa is a remarkable Islamic institution that is famous for its intricate tile work, carved cedar wood, and serene courtyard. It is a stunning illustration of the Merinid design aesthetic.

Chouara Tannery:

The Chouara Tannery is one of the world's oldest tanneries; here, you can see the process of tanning leather traditionally. The terraces that surround the tannery provide a unique vantage point from which to take in this location's arresting color palette and pungent odor, both of which set it apart from other locations.

Dar Batha Museum:

The extraordinary collection of traditional Moroccan fabrics, woodwork, and ceramics can be seen in the Dar Batha Museum, which is located in a palace that dates back to the 19th century.

B. Beaches and Parks:

Although Fes is not situated on the coast itself, there are several stunning beaches and parks within a fair distance of the city, including the following:

Sadia Beach:

On the shore of the Mediterranean in Morocco lies a beach known as Sadia Beach. This beach has earned the nickname "Blue Pearl" due to the pureness and color of its waves, which are deep blue. It has a sandy coastline that is rather extensive, there are options to participate in water sports, and there are lodgings right on the beach.

Sidi Harazem Thermal Baths:

This thermal complex is a well-liked hideaway for both residents and visitors alike. It is located around 10 kilometers from Fes. Relax and relax in the natural hot springs that are surrounded by beautiful surroundings and verdant plants.

C. Hidden Gems:

Nejjarine Museum of Wooden Arts and Crafts:

This museum, which is nestled away in a wonderfully rebuilt caravanserai, showcases the advanced woodworking talents of Moroccan craftsmen. Among the displays at the museum are examples of their work. It is a treasure trove for anybody who has an art appreciation.

Jardin Jnan Sbil:

The quiet Jardin Jnan Sbil offers a peaceful sanctuary away from the chaotic hustle and bustle of the city. There are fountains, finely manicured gardens, and a large pond with colorful fish there.

Merenid Tombs:

The Merenid Tombs are situated on a hill overlooking Fes, which affords visitors breathtaking views of the city. Visit the area just before sunset for a breathtaking perspective of the city's historic skyline.

Mellah Quarter:

Learn about the Jewish community of Fes' Mellah Quarter by exploring its rich history, traditional architecture, and synagogues. Despite its lower level of popularity, it nonetheless offers a very unique cultural experience.

REMEMBER: As a city that blends history, culture and the natural beauty of its surroundings, Fes provides tourists with an amazing view into the history and culture of Morocco. Whether you want to see the city's most famous landmarks or go off the beaten path in search of hidden treasures, Fes's stunning beauty is sure to take your breath away.

4. CHEFCHAOUEN

It is well-known for its gorgeous blue-washed architecture and scenic mountain surroundings, both of which can be seen in Chefchaouen, a charming and attractive town located in the northwest of Morocco. Visitors from all over the globe are drawn to the city of Chefchaouen, often known as the "Blue Pearl," due to the hidden treasures and unique ambiance that it has.

Let's have a look at some of the hidden treasures in and around Chefchaouen, in addition to the city's most popular parks, beaches, and tourist attractions.

The Chefchaouen Medina

The medina, also known as the old town, lies in the heart of the city and is listed as a UNESCO World Heritage Site. Its meandering, narrow streets are lined with beautiful blue and white buildings, which contribute to the attraction of the city. You may enjoy a leisurely walk around the bustling markets of the medina, make stops at the local artisan shops, and see the traditional architecture of Morocco.

The Kasbah Museum

This museum, which can be found amid the medina, is an excellent resource for learning about the history and culture of the region.

The Great Mosque

The Great Mosque is a notable religious edifice in Chefchaouen and is situated in the city's center plaza. It showcases a range of things, such as musical instruments, garments, and pottery, providing visitors with a glimpse into Chefchaouen's rich past. Non-Muslims are not permitted inside the mosque; nevertheless, they are welcome to admire the wonderful structure of the mosque from the outside owing to its iconic octagonal tower, which is a well-known landmark.

Ras El Maa

Ras El Maa is a natural spring that is well-liked by both residents and tourists. The Medina is easily accessible through a leisurely walk. It offers a relaxing escape in which you may unwind and take pleasure in the serene atmosphere.

Talassemtane National Park

Talassemtane National Park is a paradise for nature enthusiasts and is located in the Rif Mountains near Chefchaouen. It is surrounded by verdant flora and flowing waterfalls. It is well-known for its abundant plant and animal life, including cork oak and cedar woods, among other natural features.

The Akchour Waterfalls

The Akchour Waterfalls are a hidden wonder worth discovering and are located approximately an hour's drive from Chefchaouen. The park offers a variety of hiking routes that provide tourists the opportunity to enjoy the beauty of nature and interact with animals. The green surroundings of Talassemtane National Park conceal a breathtaking waterfall chain that may be seen throughout the park. Hiking to the waterfalls may provide one with a memorable experience that is punctuated by awe-inspiring panoramas at various points along the trip.

Spanish Mosque

The Spanish Mosque, which is located on top of a hill overlooking Chefchaouen, provides spectacular vistas of the city as well as the countryside that surrounds it. It is the ideal spot for spending time outside, soaking in the sunset, and shooting some stunning photographs.

Although Chefchaouen is not situated on the shore itself, numerous magnificent beaches are easily accessible by automobile, including the following:

A. The coastal communities of Tetouan and Fnideq, which are around an hour's drive from Chefchaouen, provide easy access to some of the most breathtaking beaches in the Mediterranean. These beaches provide areas to swim, sunbathe, and engage in water sports.
B. One of these beaches is known as Paradise Beach (Plage de la Perle), and it is located around 40 kilometers away from Chefchaouen. Its turquoise waters and white sand coasts make it an ideal place to escape the hustle and bustle of the city for some peace.

REMEMBER: Visitors in search of a memorable tour across Morocco can find a delightful experience in Chefchaouen owing to the city's charming blue streets, rich cultural past, stunning natural beauty, and an array of local attractions.

5. THE SAHARA DESERT

A trip to the mesmerizing Sahara Desert in Morocco may provide visitors with an experience that is both unique and memorable. This desert is famous for the stunning views it offers, as well as for the rich cultural and historical heritage it preserves. It covers a large region of territory.

Let's take a look at some of the tourist destinations that the Sahara Desert has to offer, such as its beaches, parks, and hidden jewels:

Erg Chebbi

Erg Chebbi, which is located near the town of Merzouga, is consistently ranked as one of the most popular attractions in the Sahara Desert. A few of the beautiful dunes in this region reach heights of up to 150 meters, making them some of the tallest in the world. For tourists to see the breathtaking sunrises and sunsets that occur over the dunes, they may either take camel treks or 4x4 trips. Priceless are experiences such as spending the night in a traditional desert tent, listening to indigenous music, and staring up at the stars.

Zagora

Zagora is a town that dates back to the middle ages and is located on the outskirts of the Sahara Desert. In addition to serving as a passageway into the desert, it offers visitors a glimpse of the traditional Berber way of life. The well-known sign that says "Tombouctou 52 days" is one of the attractions of the site; it commemorates the medieval caravan route that went from Morocco to Timbuktu.

Todra Gorge

While Todra Gorge is considered a natural marvel, it is not technically considered to be a part of the Sahara Desert itself. Visitors may take part in a desert excursion to see the majesty of the Sahara, explore the palm groves, and visit the neighboring markets. It may be found in the eastern part of Morocco, not far from the desert. This breathtaking network of limestone canyons is a mecca for rock climbers, hikers, and those who just appreciate nature. The sharp contrast between the dry landscape and other features, such as the towering cliffs, the clear river, and the verdant flora, provides an experience that is hard to forget.

Merzouga Beach

Despite the fact that beaches are not often associated with the Sahara Desert, Merzouga Beach is a rare and beautiful find. It is similar to a desert beach in that it is a little oasis that is surrounded by vast dunes. Its location is not far from the Erg Chebbi dunes. Tourists may relax to the sound of the lapping waves of the seasonal lake while taking in the serenity of their surroundings.

Tazzarine

Tazzarine is a modest village off the beaten path that offers a real Saharan experience. It is well-known for the stunning beauty of its landscape, which consists of rocky hills, plains with red-eared grass, and vast stretches covered in palm groves.

The Hidden Oasis of Fint

The hidden oasis of Fint offers a pleasant respite from the heat of the desert and is situated in the Atlas Mountains, not far from Ouarzazate. Getting to know the friendly locals and seeing how people continue to live in the desert in their traditional ways may be a very exciting trip. This lovely oasis is characterized by its rocky topography, which is broken up by palm trees, gardens, and a little river.

Jebel Sahro Mountain

The Jebel Sahro Mountain range is a less well-known mountain range that provides tourists with a different view over the Sahara Desert. Tourists may go on a climb, relax, or have a typical Moroccan dinner at one of the local guesthouses while observing the beautiful surroundings.

6. THE ATLAS MOUNTAINS

To the southeast of the High Atlas Mountains is where you'll find it. It is easily recognizable because of its jagged peaks, deep gorges, and expansive plateaus. The Atlas Mountains provide the ideal setting for physically demanding hikes and climbing excursions, during which visitors have the opportunity to get up close and personal with the diverse plant and animal life of the area. The beautiful Atlas Mountains are located in Morocco and cross the borders of Morocco, Algeria, and Tunisia over a distance of around 2,500 kilometers (1,550 miles). These mountains are located to the northwest of the nation and completely ring the country. At this natural marvel, visitors may take part in a variety of exciting cultural activities in addition to engaging in a broad variety of activities outside in the fresh air.

The following is a description of the Atlas Mountains, as well as some of the well-known tourist sites, beaches, parks, and unknown treasures that can be found in the area:

High Atlas Mountains:

Mount Toubkal, located in the High Atlas Mountains, is an astounding 4,167 meters (13,671 feet) tall and is the range's highest peak.

Toubkal National Park

Toubkal National Park is a haven for those who are passionate about the environment and is located in the High Atlas Mountains. It attracts a large number of hikers and mountaineers who take pleasure in tackling difficult journeys.

Ourika Valley

A day excursion to the lovely Ourika Valley is one of the most popular things to do while visiting Marrakech. It is home to the famous Mount Toubkal and has opportunities for trekking, seeing animals, and taking in amazing panoramic views. The landscape is breathtaking, and there is a plethora of plant life, as well as traditional Berber towns and thundering waterfalls.

Ait Ben Haddou

Ait Ben Haddou is a walled village that is located on the southern slopes of the High Atlas Mountains and is a UNESCO World Heritage Site. Visitors may enjoy a leisurely trek or embark on a foot tour of the valley. In addition to this, it is famous for the kasbahs, or fortified residences, that have been preserved there. These kasbahs have been featured in many movies, including "Gladiator" and "Game of Thrones."

High Atlas Dades Gorges

The Dades Gorges in the High Atlas Mountains are home to towering cliffs, winding roads, and the picturesque Dades River, all of which contribute to the area's jaw-dropping splendor. Rock climbing, hiking, and just soaking in the amazing rock formations are popular activities that people enjoy doing at this place.

Ouzoud Falls

The Ouzoud Falls are the tallest waterfalls in all of Morocco, and they can be found in the Middle Atlas Mountains. Visitors have the option of taking a walk to the bottom of the falls, going on boat trips, or just sitting and staring at the rushing waters while surrounded by verdant foliage. In addition to its picturesque old town, which boasts winding alleyways, blue-painted houses, and a lively port, it is home to several beautiful beaches.

Ifrane

Ifrane is a treasure in the Middle Atlas Mountains due to its alpine-like position and unusual architecture. It is frequently referred to as "Little Switzerland," which is a nickname for the city. There, you can find the campus of Al Akhawayn University, as well as well-maintained gardens and a medina that is styled after those seen in Europe.

Paradise Valley

Paradise Valley is a hidden haven that may be found near Agadir in the foothills of the High Atlas Mountains. The profusion of natural swimming pools, beautiful waterfalls, and picturesque hiking paths make it a sanctuary of tranquility for those who have a deep appreciation for the natural world.

Amizmiz

Amizmiz is a typical Berber town that is found in the foothills of the High Atlas Mountains. It is well-known for its bustling weekly market, which is where residents get together to trade products and crafts with one another. It offers the possibility of learning about genuine culture and gaining exposure to Berber traditions.

REMEMBER: The Atlas Mountains in Morocco provide a broad range of activities, from arduous mountain excursions to peaceful valleys and unknown gems. These mountains may be found in Morocco. Every visitor, regardless of their interests, will have a good time in this region, whether they seek natural beauty, opportunities for cultural immersion, or outdoor activities.

7. CITY OF RABAT

Rabat, the lively and historically important capital of Morocco, is home to a wide range of cultural activities, stunning beaches, verdant parks, and hidden jewels that are just waiting to be found. The following is a description of the beaches, parks, and other tourist attractions located in Rabat, as well as a few hidden spots:

A. Tourist Highlights:

The Majestic Mohammed V Mausoleum:

The majestic Mohammed V Mausoleum is located close to the unfinished Hassan Tower, which is a tall tower.

The Kasbah of the Udayas:

The Kasbah of the Udayas is an ancient fortification that features breathtaking views of the Atlantic Ocean, meandering alleyways, and white and blue structures. UNESCO has designated this location as a World Heritage Site. It is the best place in the city to immerse oneself in the city's long and illustrious past.

Royal Palace:

Even though the general public is not permitted inside, Rabat's Royal Palace is widely regarded as one of the world's greatest architectural achievements. Visitors get the opportunity to take in the ornate walls, gateways, and gates that surround the royal compound.

Chellah Necropolis:

Chellah Necropolis is a place that is both tranquil and enigmatic, and it is the site of old Roman and medieval relics. It provides a peaceful escape from the hustle and bustle of the city with its beautiful gardens, intricate mosaics, and ancient tombs.

B. Beaches:

Plage de Rabat:

This sandy beach can be found along the Atlantic coast, and it is the perfect area to have some leisure time and unwind. Visitors have access to several different water activities, as well as the opportunity to sunbathe and swim.

Plage des Nations:

This beach, which is located close to the heart of the city, is well-liked by both residents of the area and tourists. On the beach, there are several restaurants and cafés where you can indulge in some mouthwatering Moroccan cuisine. The atmosphere is bustling.

C. Parks:

The Andalusian Gardens:

The Andalusian Gardens are a beautiful park that has architecture inspired by the Moors, as well as a variety of bright flowers and peaceful fountains.

The Jardin d'Essais Botaniques:

The Jardin d'Essais Botaniques, popularly known as the Botanical Gardens, is a large green oasis with a diverse variety of plants, including exotic species from different parts of Morocco. It is the ideal spot for a relaxing walk amid nature and to decompress. Those who have a passion for being outside will find this location to be ideal.

D. Hidden Gems:

The Oudaias Museum:

This unassuming museum is nestled away in the Kasbah of the Udayas. It has a collection of Moroccan arts and crafts, traditional clothing, and antiquities.

Villa des Arts:

Villa des Arts is a venue for contemporary art in a gorgeous neighborhood that often hosts exhibits and other cultural events. It gives visitors a glimpse into the nation's rich cultural heritage. It is a secret gem for individuals who are interested in contemporary art from Morocco.

Mellah:

Mellah is Rabat's hidden Jewish district, and it gives a view into the city's diverse history. As you navigate the twisting alleys and pay a visit to the synagogue, you will get the opportunity to learn about the unique combination of Jewish and Moroccan culture.

REMEMBER: Rabat, with its historic monuments, stunning beaches, lovely parks, and hidden jewels, provides a mesmerizing experience for travelers who are searching for a combination of history, nature, and exploration in their vacation destination.

8. ASILAH

Asilah is a picture-perfect coastal town in northern Morocco that is famous for the allure of its medina, the splendor of its beaches, and the vitality of its artist community. Because it provides a one-of-a-kind combination of historical architecture, cultural legacy, and natural beauty, it is a well-liked destination for vacationers. The following is a list of some of the most popular tourist attractions, beaches, parks, and hidden treasures that can be found in Asilah:

Asilah's Medina:

The Medina of Asilah is located in the heart of the city and is characterized by its twisting and serpentine lanes, whitewashed buildings, vibrant murals, and lively marketplaces.

Walls and Gates:

The medina in Asilah is enclosed by walls and gates that have been well maintained and give spectacular views of the town and the Atlantic Ocean. This makes it a joy to walk around the medina and take in its traditional stores, art galleries, and cafés. The most famous gate is Bab Homar, which is also the main entrance to the medina. Bab Homar has been around for centuries.

Asilah Beach:

Asilah is known for its stunning coastline as well as its pristine beaches. The principal beach is called Plage d'Asilah, and it is a long sandy stretch where you can relax, work on your tan, and take invigorating dives in the Atlantic Ocean.

Paradise Beach:

Paradise Beach is a hidden treasure that is near Asilah and provides a setting that is more serene and private than other beaches in the area. In addition to being an excellent spot for a variety of water activities, including swimming, surfing, and others, this spot is also fantastic for viewing the sunset.

El-Hoceima National Park:

Although it is not physically situated in the city of Asilah, El-Hoceima National Park is not far away and is well deserving of a trip. It is well known that this protected region is home to rugged mountains, dense woods, and pristine beaches. Picnicking, hiking, and seeing various species of animals are just some of the activities that can be done at this outdoor enthusiast's paradise.

Centre Hassan II:

Centre Hassan II, the town's major plaza, is a lively meeting location surrounded by cafés, restaurants, and shops.

Asilah:

Asilah is home to a strong artistic community, which is on full display during August's annual Asilah Arts Festival. This location is an excellent spot to relax, people-watch, and get a feel for the spirit of the area. The walls of this village are covered with stunning murals that have been created by local, national, and even worldwide artists. The museums, art galleries, and other types of cultural facilities regularly host a large number of different kinds of exhibits and events.

Portuguese Cistern:

The Portuguese Cistern is a well-kept secret in Asilah. It is an underground water storage facility that dates back to the 15th century. The high ceilings and slim columns that make up its architectural plan contribute to the building's allure.

Asilah's Archeological Museum:

The Archeological Museum in Asilah is home to a range of artifacts and exhibits that provide insight into the history of the town as well as ancient civilizations. The public is invited to attend art exhibitions and other activities that are conducted in the cistern. If you are interested in the long history of the region, this is an excellent location to visit.

Asilah:

The town of Asilah is well-known for its quaint cafés and restaurants, many of which serve mouthwatering Moroccan food, most notably fresh fish. Do not miss the opportunity to indulge in the food of the area while taking in the breathtaking views of the ocean.

REMEMBER: Tourists will find Asilah to be captivating owing to the city's interesting history, stunning beaches, and thriving art scene. Whether you want to wander the winding alleyways of the medina, rest on the sandy beaches, or immerse yourself in the town's cultural treasures, Asilah is sure to leave an indelible mark on you.

9. CASABLANCA

The most modern of Morocco's cities, Casablanca, is also home to some of the country's most important historical landmarks. Casablanca is the country's financial and economic hub, and it is also home to many popular tourist destinations, including breathtaking beaches, parks that are enchanted, and hidden gems.

Let's have a look at some of the most famous landmarks and attractions in the city:

The Hassan II Mosque

The Hassan II Mosque is widely regarded as one of the finest examples of Islamic architecture and is among the world's largest mosques. Because of its superb architecture, lavish ornamentation, and breathtaking location overlooking the Atlantic Ocean, it is an absolute must-see attraction.

The Old Medina:

To get a feel for Casablanca's genuine allure, take a stroll through the narrow alleys of the Old Medina.

Corniche:

The picturesque seaside promenade known as the Corniche is a perfect spot to enjoy a leisurely walk or go for a bike ride. Here, you can immerse yourself in the bustling souks (markets), where you can buy vibrant fabrics, spices, and traditional Moroccan crafts. The Corniche is home to some of the best restaurants and cafés in the area, as well as hotels with five stars and spectacular views of the water. It's a wonderful spot to chill.

Ain Diab Beach:

Ain Diab Beach is a holiday destination that is well-liked by both the residents and the visitors who visit the area. Its location is just next to the Corniche. With its soft sand, crystal blue seas, and a wide range of beachfront clubs and restaurants, this location is ideal for unwinding and taking in some rays of sunshine.

Parc de la Ligue Arabe:

Parc de la Ligue Arabe is a verdant haven in the heart of the city that provides a serene escape from the hustle and bustle of the surrounding area. The Parc de la Ligue Arabe has well-kept gardens, fountains, and shady areas that are perfect for picnics and strolls. The grounds are also well maintained.

Anfa District:

Take a leisurely walk through the upscale Anfa District, which is well-known for its luxurious residences, upscale eating places, and chic shopping businesses.

Museum of Moroccan Judaism:

Explore the Museum of Moroccan Judaism to delve into the rich Jewish history of Morocco. This attraction offers a wonderful opportunity to engage with the contemporary and global aspects of Casablanca.

The Shrine of Sidi Abderrahman:

The Shrine of Sidi Abderrahman provides a serene and mystical atmosphere, showcasing an array of artifacts, photographs, and exhibits that offer insights into the Moroccan Jewish heritage. Situated on a secluded rocky islet not far from the coastline, this hidden gem is a cherished destination for both locals and tourists, who visit to reflect and admire the stunning ocean views.

Quartier Habous:

Quartier Habous is an area that combines Moroccan and French architectural styles. It is also known as the "New Medina," and this name is occasionally given to it.

La Sqala:

La Sqala is a historic fortress that has been converted into a restaurant and is located close to the Old Medina. It is a wonderful spot to buy local goods, enjoy Moroccan cuisine, and learn about the culture. Because of its enchanting garden setting, mouthwatering Moroccan cuisine, and unique atmosphere, it is a well-kept secret that is perfect for eating and relaxing.

REMEMBER: The city's lively environment, historical buildings, and hidden gems make it an alluring destination for tourists who are looking for a blend of contemporary and history in their vacation spot.

10. MEKNES

Meknes is a city located in northern Morocco that is home to a significant amount of cultural history. It has a rich history that dates back to the 11th century and was once the capital of the country at one point in time. Meknes, which is well-known for its restored medieval architecture and enticing ambiance, offers a range of tourist attractions, some of which include magnificent monuments, intriguing museums, and hidden treasures. Meknes is located in the country of Morocco. Meknes has a large number of parks and gardens, which helps to make up for the fact that it is not located on the coast and, hence, does not have any beaches. Let's have a look at some of the most impressive landmarks and hidden treasures that Meknes has to offer:

The Bab Mansour Gate:

The Bab Mansour Gate is a magnificent entrance to the ancient medina of Meknes and is considered to be one of the most impressive gates in all of Morocco. Because of its magnificent appearance and wonderful construction, it is an absolute must-see location.

Heri es-Souani:

Sultan Moulay Ismail oversaw the construction of this enormous granary and stable complex. Its expansive courtyards and enormous underground rooms offer an insight into the sultan's ambitious architectural endeavors.

Place El-Hedim:

This vibrant plaza is the core of Meknes. It is located just across from Bab Mansour. It is a great place to have some Moroccan street cuisine while people watching and taking in the bustling atmosphere.

Meknes Medina:

Walk through the Meknes Medina, which has been designated a UNESCO World Heritage Site. The streets are quite small and twisty. This neighborhood gives a genuine experience of Morocco with its traditional markets, artisan workshops, and historic mosques.

The Dar Jamai Museum:

The Dar Jamai Museum showcases a range of Moroccan artwork, including pottery, jewelry, textiles, and woodwork, inside a wonderfully restored palace. In addition to this, it provides some insight into the history and culture of Meknes.

The Moulay Idriss Mausoleum:

This mausoleum is considered a center of pilgrimage for Muslims since it is the last resting place of Moulay Idriss I, who established the first Islamic state in Morocco. It creates an environment that is conducive to calmness and meditation.

Bou Inania Madrasa:

This splendid theological institution was built in the 14th century and is known as the Bou Inania Madrasa. It is well-known for its intricate tile work, carved wood, and attractive courtyard. This little-known fact brings to light the breathtaking architecture that can be seen in Meknes.

Moulay Ismail Mausoleum

Sultan Moulay Ismail was laid to rest at the Moulay Ismail Mausoleum, which can be found just next to Bab Mansour.

Jardin Lahboul:

At the quiet Jardin Lahboul, you may get away from the rush and bustle of the city. It features gorgeous green tiles and peaceful furniture. The lush vegetation, beautiful fountains, and peaceful atmosphere make this the ideal place for a relaxed walk.

11. VOLUBILIS

The ancient Roman city of Volubilis may be found in modern-day Morocco. It is famous for both its historical and archaeological value. Because of its location close to the city of Meknes and the fact that it is a UNESCO globe Heritage Site, it is frequented by visitors from all over the globe.

The following is a description of Volubilis, covering its most popular tourist attractions, adjacent beaches, and parks, as well as several lesser-known but impressive features:

A. Tourist Highlights:

Roman ruins:

The Roman ruins at Volubilis are known for being exceptionally well-preserved and for providing visitors with a glimpse into the majesty of the old capital. Basilicas, triumphal arches, elaborately patterned mosaic floors, and remnants of Roman temples are some of the attractions that tourists may see in Volubilis.

The Capitol:

One of the most magnificent monuments in Volubilis is the Capitol, which is devoted to the three principal Roman deities, Jupiter, Juno, and Minerva.

The **"House of Orpheus"**:

The "House of Orpheus" house in Volubilis is covered with superb mosaics that portray scenes from Roman mythology. • The church next door contains gorgeous columns and intricate sculptures. A reminder of the long-standing legacy of creative expression in the city is provided by the elaborate designs and superior workmanship of the product.

B. Parks and Hidden Gems:

Moulay Idriss Zerhoun:

The settlement of Moulay Idriss Zerhoun, which is located nearby and is perched on a hill, is often regarded as the holiest pilgrimage site in all of Morocco.

Zerhoun Blue Spring:

Zerhoun Blue Spring is a natural spring with crystalline blue water that is near Moulay Idriss Zerhoun. Moulay Idriss Zerhoun's winding alleys, whitewashed houses, and spectacular vistas provide a one-of-a-kind look into the culture and history of Morocco. As a result of the serene atmosphere and beautiful scenery, this spot is ideal for having a picnic or going for a swim to cool down.

NOTE: The captivating atmosphere of Volubilis is due in no little part to the city's rich history, picturesque surroundings, and convenient access to area attractions. An excursion to this historic site and the area around it provides tourists with a wide range of opportunities for personal growth and development. Guests may learn about the region's rich history by exploring the ancient Roman ruins, after which they can relax on the area's beautiful beaches or hunt for buried treasure.

12. THE MERZOUGA

Merzouga is a little community in the southeast of Morocco that is well-known for the breathtaking desert vistas and fascinating adventures that may be had there. Its location on the edge of the Sahara Desert makes it possible to experience a one-of-a-kind combination of the region's natural splendor, cultural history, and exciting activities. The following is a summary of Merzouga, covering its most popular tourist attractions, the beaches and parks located nearby, and its lesser-known charms:

Lake Dayet Srji:

Lake Dayet Srji is a serene oasis amid the desert that is conveniently located near Merzouga. This temporary lake, together with its breathtaking surroundings and many options for bird watching, serves as a magnet for a wide range of migratory bird species. It is a perfect setting for relaxing, having a picnic, or enjoying a leisurely walk while taking in the tranquil surroundings.

Khamlia:

Located close to Merzouga is a little town known as Khamlia, which is famous for its colorful Gnawa culture and music. The Gnawa people are indigenous to sub-Saharan Africa and are famous for their peculiar musical style as well as the religious traditions that they follow. Visitors may take in performances that are full of heart, learn about Gnawa traditions, and thoroughly immerse themselves in the vibrant atmosphere of this welcoming hamlet.

Rissani:

Rissani, the nearest settlement to Merzouga, is not only an important historical center but also a place with a rich cultural past. It was a key commercial station along the ancient caravan routes, and the historic architecture and crowded souks (markets) there still bore evidence of its famous history (markets). Do not miss the chance to indulge in some of the local delicacies, such as Madfouna and Medfouna (stuffed bread), while taking a leisurely walk around the lively market.

C. Hidden Gems:

Tafilalt Oasis:

During your exploration of Merzouga, you may want to consider venturing away from the main roads to unearth some hidden gems. One of these hidden gems is the Tafilalt Oasis, a verdant palm forest that stretches over the desert. It is a tranquil sanctuary where you may amble around at your own pace while basking in the shade of the palm trees.

Maadid Dunes:

The Maadid Dunes may be found some distance to the north of Merzouga. These dunes are yet another unknown treasure that offers visitors a desert experience that is more tranquil and isolated.

13. OUARZAZATE

Ouarzazate, located in the south of Morocco, is a mesmerizing city that is sometimes referred to as the "Hollywood of Morocco." It is well-known since it is considered the "Gateway to the Desert." It provides a one-of-a-kind combination of attractiveness stemming from the film industry, a rich cultural past, and breathtaking natural beauty. The following is a list of some of the most popular tourist spots in and around Ouarzazate, including parks, beaches, and other attractions.

Atlas Film Studios:

Ouarzazate is home to Atlas Film Studios, which holds the title of the largest film studio in all of Africa. By going on a tour, you may see the fascinating settings that were used in the filming of popular movies such as "Gladiator," "Lawrence of Arabia," and "Game of Thrones," among others.

Taourirt Kasbah:

Pay a visit to the spectacular Taourirt Kasbah, a fortress that was originally owned by the Glaoui family. It is a joy to explore because of the beautiful architecture, winding lanes, and traditional Moroccan furniture that can be found there.

Draa Valley:

Take a leisurely drive through this beautiful valley, which is well-known for its date palm trees, old ksars (fortified towns), and breathtaking landscape. The valley gives opportunities for camel rides, trekking, and exposure to traditional Berber culture.

Tifoultoute Kasbah:

The Tifoultoute Kasbah, which is built on a hill overlooking Ouarzazate, provides breathtaking views of the city as well as its natural surroundings.

Lake Mansour Edddahbi:

Lake Mansour Edddahbi is a gorgeous reservoir near Ouarzazate; nevertheless, it does not have any beaches associated with it. The wonderful architecture of the Kasbah has a rich historical value. It provides an atmosphere that is perfect for relaxation and private picnics due to its peaceful atmosphere and breathtaking landscapes.

Skoura Oasis:

Located around 40 kilometers away from Ouarzazate, Skoura Oasis is well-known for its lush palm trees, historic kasbahs, and peaceful atmosphere.

The Amridil Kasbah:

The Amridil Kasbah, which can be found in the Skoura Oasis, is one of the most famous kasbahs in all of Morocco. Take your time and enjoy the peaceful ambiance as you stroll gently around the oasis. Classical interiors, well-preserved architecture, and lovely gardens all contribute to creating a building that offers a glimpse into the history and culture of Morocco.

14. TANGIER

Tangier, located in northern Morocco, is a flourishing city with a rich history that has been shaped by a variety of diverse cultural influences. Tangier, known as the "Gateway to Africa," has been attracting writers, artists, and adventurers for centuries due to its reputation as a cultural melting pot.

The following is a list of the tourist attractions that Tangier has to offer, including its beaches, parks, and some hidden treasures to uncover:

A. Tourist Highlights:

The Kasbah:

The Kasbah is an ancient fortress with winding pathways, exquisite architecture, and spectacular views of the Mediterranean Sea. It is one of the most popular tourist attractions in Marrakech. It is a wonderful location from which to begin your exploration of the ancient town.

Medina:

Lose yourself in the vibrant Medina of Tangier, where you can stroll through colorful marketplaces, purchase products that have been created, and experience food from the area.

Tangier American Legation Museum:

Pay a visit to the Tangier American Legation Museum, which is the only historical site associated with the United States that can be found located outside of the nation. It has an impressive assortment of artwork, vintage records, and exhibits that bring attention to the special relationship that exists between Morocco and the United States.

Caves of Hercules:

The Caves of Hercules may be reached from the city in a very short amount of time by car. It is reported that Hercules took pauses from his labors in these ancient caverns in the natural environment. The caverns provide mesmerizing views of the Atlantic Ocean as well as spectacular rock formations.

B. Beaches:

Plage Malabata:

Plage Malabata in Tangier is a well-liked beach that has great beaches, water that is crystal clear, and a lively scene all around it.

Achakkar Beach:

Achakkar Beach is a hidden jewel that is known for its quiet and tranquility. It is a wonderful spot to relax, take in the sunlight, and participate in water sports like swimming and jet skiing. It is located on the outskirts of the main city area. Because it is surrounded by cliffs and untamed landscapes, it provides a peaceful haven in which one may take in the splendor of the natural world as well as a chance to do so.

C. Parks:

Perdicaris Park:

Tucked away in the hills above Tangier is a beautiful green region called Perdicaris Park. This park is home to a wide variety of rare flora and animals.

Mendoubia Gardens:

Mendoubia Gardens is a calm oasis with gorgeous gardens, fountains, and palm trees that are near the Grand Socco area. Enjoy a picnic while enjoying a leisurely walk around the meandering pathways of the park and taking in the panoramic views of the city and the Strait of Gibraltar. It is the perfect setting for relaxing, reading a book, or sipping a cup of tea in quiet, all of which may be done in this place.

D. Hidden Gems:

Café Hafa:

For years, singers, authors, and artists have flocked to the world-famous café known as Café Hafa.

Marshan:

Discover the charming Marshan area, with its picture-perfect white buildings and meandering lanes, while sipping scrumptious mint tea while reclining on a rock overlooking the beach. It provides stunning vistas, a bohemian vibe, and delicious views of the ocean.

Petit Socco:

Petit Socco is a busy district in the middle of Medina that is a flourishing hub for local craftsmen, street traders, and cafes. You may enjoy a leisurely walk through the art galleries, hidden cafés, and calm environs that can be found here. It is a wonderful spot to take in the liveliness of Tangier, indulge in some of the region's delectable food, and look for one-of-a-kind souvenirs.

15. AGADIR

The city of Agadir is located on the western coast of Morocco and is a popular tourist destination due to its stunning beaches, pleasant climate, and significant cultural past. The following is a description of Agadir, including some of its lesser-known beaches, parks, and other places of interest to tourists:

A. Tourist Highlights:

Agadir Beach:

The vicinity is ideal for water-based activities, swimming, and sunbathing because of its scenic coastline and lengthy stretch of sandy beaches.

Kasbah of Agadir Oufella:

Agadir and its environs are visible from the Kasbah of Agadir Oufella. In addition, there is a little museum nearby that focuses on the history of the area and displays relics.

Souk El Had:

The bustling Souk El Had is a genuine treasure trove of Moroccan trinkets, clothes, spices, and handicrafts. The market is known as "The Gold Market." Visitors get the opportunity to purchase one-of-a-kind items while taking in the vibrant atmosphere.

La Médina d'Agadir:

This reconstructed medina provides visitors with an opportunity to see traditional Moroccan architecture and craftsmanship. It is home to a wide selection of shops, restaurants, and places of cultural significance.

Valley of the Birds:

This is a bird park that is located very near the heart of the city and is home to a wide variety of avian species, including flamingos, parrots, and peacocks, among others. It is the perfect place to go to get away from the hustle and bustle of the city.

B. Beaches:

Plage d'Agadir:

Plage d'Agadir, the most popular beach in Agadir, is around ten kilometers long, has golden sand that is perfectly flawless, completely transparent seas, and first-rate services and facilities for those who visit the beach.

Insurance Beach:

Insurance Beach is recognized for its wild beauty, featuring cliffs, caves, and natural rock formations.

Taghazout Beach:

Taghazout Beach, which is situated just to the north of Agadir, is a gorgeous beach that is well-liked by surfers due to the consistency of its waves and the laid-back atmosphere. It may be found to the south of Agadir. It is an ideal spot for sightseeing as well as lounging in the sun.

C. Parks & Gardens:

Jardin de Olhao:

The Jardin de Olhao, located in the heart of Agadir, is a peaceful haven that offers a variety of unusual plant species, dense foliage, and calming water elements. It is the perfect place for a leisurely walk or a picnic in the park.

Ibn Zaidoun Park:

Ibn Zaidoun Park is a park featuring well-kept plants, play spaces, and a lake with pedal boats. It is located adjacent to the marina. The region is commonly visited by groups consisting of families and those who like being outside.

Sous-Massa National Park:

Those who have a deep appreciation for the natural world will find the Sous-Massa National Park to be a veritable paradise not too far from Agadir. It is home to a vast diversity of avian, mammalian, and reptilian species due to the many ecosystems that it has, such as marshes, forests, and cliffs along the coast.

D. Hidden Gems:

Tafraoute:

This little village is situated in the Anti-Atlas Mountains, and it is known for its unusual scenery of pink granite rocks. Visitors have the opportunity to learn about the Berber culture while hiking through almond trees and exploring the adjacent valleys.

Tiout Oasis:

Tiout Oasis is a serene oasis that is located near the town of Taroudant. It is characterized by the presence of palm trees as well as traditional mud-brick buildings. Relaxation, authentic Moroccan food, and donkey rides through the palm groves are all fantastic activities that may be enjoyed at this place.

16. TÉTOUAN

Tétouan, which is located in the north of Morocco, is a fascinating city that is well-known for its rich history, exquisite architecture, and picturesque surroundings. Tétouan, often known as the "White Dove," is a location in Morocco that is unlike any other due to its combination of Moroccan and Spanish characteristics.

Tétouan's Medina:

Tétouan's Medina, which has been acknowledged by UNESCO, is located in the middle of the city and is a maze of twisting streets, lively marketplaces, and gorgeous architecture in the Andalusian style. Tétouan's beaches, parks, and unknown treasures include the following:

Beaches:

Tétouan's stretch of coastline along the Mediterranean has a plethora of beautiful beaches. One of the most well-known is Martil Beach, which is noted for having beautiful golden beaches, seas that are crystal clear, and a busy promenade that runs down the beachfront. Other well-known beaches that provide a peaceful retreat to the coast are Cabo Negro Beach and M'diq Beach.

La Muralla Park:

La Muralla Park is a peaceful green refuge that is adjacent to the Medina and gives relaxation from the bustling metropolis. The park provides visitors with stunning vistas of the mountains in the vicinity, as well as pathways for walking and abundant floral displays. It is an ideal spot for a picnic or a walk in the park.

A. Hidden Gems:

El Jebha:

El Jebha is a charming fishing town that is a hidden gem that is worth exploring. It is situated approximately 30 kilometers from Tétouan. Because of its pristine beaches, crystal clear waters, and laid-back vibe, this destination is ideal for anyone searching for a peaceful getaway by the water.

Teti Tleta:

Teti Tleta is a picturesque village that can be found tucked away in the Rif Mountains. It is only a short drive away from Tétouan. This undiscovered treasure provides a one-of-a-kind opportunity to submerge oneself in the natural splendor of the surrounding area. It is famous for its hiking trails, the traditional Berber culture it preserves, and its stunning environment.

Smir Park:

The nearby community of M'diq is home to the family-friendly amusement park known as Smir Park, which features a variety of rides, attractions, and a water park for guests of all ages. It is a wonderful choice for a fun day excursion, and it is highly recommended if you are traveling with children.

17. EL JADIDAH

El Jadida is a picturesque coastal city in Morocco that is recognized for its extensive history, spectacular architecture, and beautiful beaches. It is located on the Atlantic coast of Morocco. The following is a description of El Jadida, including its most popular tourist attractions, beaches, and parks, as well as some of its best-kept secrets:

A. Tourist Highlights:

Portuguese Cistern:

The Portuguese Cistern, also known as the Cistern of El Jadida, is a spectacular underground water storage facility that was built during the time that Portugal occupied Morocco. It is characterized by a variety of columns and arches, both of which lend it a characteristic air.

Portuguese City Walls:

The Portuguese city walls that were built around El Jadida in the 16th century are still standing and in fair condition. Visitors are welcome to walk along the walls, which provide breathtaking vistas of the surrounding area, including the city and the ocean.

El Jadida Citadel:

The El Jadida Citadel, often referred to as the Mazagan Fortification, is a fortification that dates back to the Middle Ages and is on the UNESCO World Heritage List. It provides visitors with beautiful views of the coastline as well as a glimpse into the history of the city.

El Jadida:

Explore the historic quarter of El Jadida, known as the Medina. It is characterized by winding streets that are lined with traditional homes, local boutiques, and cafes. Discover authentic Moroccan culture and indulge in the region's delicious food by taking advantage of the opportunities offered by the Medina.

B. Beaches:

Sidi Bouzid Beach:

Sidi Bouzid Beach is a well-known beach that is near the heart of the city and features powdery white sand and waters that are remarkably clear. It is a fantastic place to go swimming, sunbathing, and participate in a variety of water sports.

Haouzia Beach:

Haouzia Beach is a beach that is less frequented and is known for its tranquility. It is located a few kilometers south of El

Jadida. It is perfect for spending the day lounging by the lake or going on a long walk along the shoreline.

C. Parks & Gardens:

The Mohammed V Park:

The Mohammed V Park is a serene haven that features gorgeous landscaping, fountains, and abundant plant life. It is located smack dab amid the bustling metropolis. It is the ideal location for going on strolls and having picnics.

D. Hidden Gems:

Mazagan Golf Club:

Guests staying at the Mazagan Beach Resort have access to the 18-hole Mazagan Golf Club, where they can enjoy a round of golf throughout their stay. It features spectacular views of the ocean in addition to a round of golf that is both difficult and exciting.

Oualidia Lagoon:

Even though it is located outside of El Jadida itself, the Oualidia Lagoon is nonetheless conveniently close and warrants a visit. It is well-known for its picturesque lagoon and is a sanctuary for birdwatching, water sports, and feasting on local seafood.

Portuguese Cemetery:

The Portuguese Cemetery is tucked away on a hillside overlooking the city and provides a tranquil and contemplative atmosphere. It's a well-kept secret that provides a fresh perspective on El Jadida's history, yet nobody knows about it.

CHAPTER FOUR
10 EXCITING OUTDOOR
ADVENTURES TO EXPERIENCE

When embarking on a journey to Morocco, a world of outdoor adventures awaits, each offering a glimpse into the nation's diverse landscapes and cultural heritage.

Below is a selection of ten unmissable outdoor activities in Morocco, paired with their associated top tourist destinations:

1. MARKET EXPLORATION

While you are exploring the Medina, make your way through the winding streets of the old Medina in Marrakech, which is a UNESCO World Heritage site. Enjoy the bustling atmosphere, visit the well-known Jemaa el-Fnaa plaza, and haggle for deals at the traditional marketplace (souks).

2. HIKING

Begin your tour across the majestic Atlas Mountains on foot so you may fully appreciate their beauty. Discover breathtaking routes, take in the awe-inspiring scenery of the surrounding mountains, and become familiar with the Berber communities in the area. The Ourika Valley and Toubkal National Park are two of the most popular destinations for hikers in Morocco.

3. CAMEL RIDING

Travel to the immense Sahara Desert, which is located close to the town of Merzouga, and ride a camel through the desert to experience the mystique of this pastime. Spend the night in a traditional Bedouin camp under the starry desert sky, explore the interesting dunes, and see a breathtaking sunrise or sunset.

4. EXPLORE LOCAL ARTS AND PHOTOGRAPHS

Travel to Chefchaouen, often known as the Blue City, and wander about the mesmerizing streets that have been painted blue. This picturesque village, which can be found tucked away in the Rif Mountains, offers an atmosphere of peace and tranquility, making it a great setting for taking strolls, taking photographs, and discovering the local arts and crafts sector.

5. GO SURFING

Taghazout, located on the Atlantic coast of Morocco, is a popular destination for surfers. Think about coming there if surfing is something you enjoy doing. The consistent waves and laid-back vibe make this spot an ideal destination for surfers of all experience levels. Participate in some yoga courses or find a quiet spot on the beach to relax.

6. STUDY HISTORY

Learn more about the history of these old fortified towns by paying a visit to the Ait Ben Haddou Kasbahs. The spectacular earthen building that is part of this UNESCO World Heritage site has served as the background for several films. As you wind your way through the maze of alleys, you might pick up interesting tidbits of information about the region's long and illustrious past.

7. EXPLORE AMAZING ROCK FORMATIONS

The Todra Gorges are located in the eastern range of the High Atlas Mountains and are home to some of the most stunning scenery in all of Morocco. Take in the awe-inspiring natural beauty by going on a hike along the towering canyon walls, gazing at the amazing rock formations, and exploring the surrounding area.

8. KITESURFING SPORTS

Take some time to rest at Essaouira Beach. The fishing community of Essaouira is home to a beach that is known for its laid-back vibe. It is well renowned for having strong winds, making it an ideal location for wind and kitesurfing sports. In addition, you will have the opportunity to indulge in delectable freshly caught seafood, take languid strolls along the sandy beach, and travel to the charming medina.

9. NATURE AND BIRDWATCHING

Observing a Wide Variety of Animals at the Souss Massa National Park. The Souss Massa National Park is located close to Agadir, and it is home to many different species of animals. This protected area offers a wonderful opportunity for people who are interested in nature and birdwatching, as it is home to a wide variety of wildlife, including pink flamingos, rare bird species, wild boars, and Barbary macaques.

10. ENJOY HOT AIR BALLOON

Take a Journey in a Hot Air Balloon Over Marrakech. Taking a journey in a hot air balloon will provide you with a unique perspective of Marrakech and the surrounding area. As you ascend above the city, make sure to look out the window and take in the spectacular views of the Atlas Mountains and the Palmeraie Oasis.

REMEMBER: Your trip will be an experience you will never forget if you participate in some of these outdoor activities, which give you a taste of the beauty, culture, and excitement that Morocco has to offer.

CHAPTER FIVE
TRAVEL PLANS

The following is a step-by-step travel plan for touring Morocco over five days:

DAY 1: A VISIT TO MARRAKECH

Step 1:

Once you arrive, look for a hotel or other accommodation in the Marrakech area.

Step 2:

Start the day by going to the famous Jemaa el-Fnaa plaza as well as the medina, which is located in the old part of Marrakech.

Step 3:

Stroll around the crowded souks (markets) and indulge in as much retail therapy as your heart desires.

Step 4:

Take in the stunning architecture and beautiful grounds that the Bahia Palace has to offer.

Step 5:

In the evening, make your way to Marrakech to partake in a typical Moroccan meal and soak up the city's electric vibe.

DAY 2: A VISIT TO ATLAS MOUNTAINS AND ESSAOUIRA

Step 1:

Spend a day in the Atlas Mountains, which are conveniently located near Marrakech.

Step 2:

If you want to see some breathtaking sights, you could go to the lovely Ourika Valley.

Step 3:

Learn about the indigenous Berber way of life and visit some traditional Berber settlements.

Step 4:

Spend the afternoon in Essaouira, a town located along the coast.

Step 5:

Explore the medina, which is on the list of World Heritage Sites maintained by UNESCO, and enjoy the laid-back atmosphere of this coastal town.

Step 6:

Also, don't miss the chance to have some deliciously fresh fish.

DAY 3: A TRIP TO FES

Step1:

Pay a visit to the famous Al-Qarawiyyin University and Mosque, which is one of the oldest universities in the world.

Step 2:

Explore Fes' tanneries to learn more about the traditional method of creating leather.

Step 3:

Explore the maze-like streets and vibrant markets of the UNESCO-listed Fes el-Bali medina.

Step 4:

Visit the city of Fes, which is one of the most ancient and fascinating cities in Morocco.

Step 5:

Finish off the day by dining at one of the rooftop restaurants and taking in the breathtaking views of the city below.

DAY 4: A VISIT TO CHEFCHAOUEN

Step 1:

Try to spend the day at Chefchaouen, well known as the "Blue City," which is located in the Rif Mountains.

Step 2:

Take in the splendor of your surroundings as you meander along the winding alleys that have been painted blue.

Step 3:

Pay a visit to the Kasbah Museum to learn more about the history of the region.

Step 4:

Climbing on the mountains that surround the town will reward you with stunning panoramas of the area.

Step5:

While relaxing in one of the charming cafes, treat yourself to a traditional cup of Moroccan mint tea and savor the flavor.

DAY 5: VISITING CASABLANCA AND DEPARTING

Step1:

Plan a trip to Casablanca, which is both the nation's capital and its largest city.

Step 2:

The Hassan II Mosque is renowned for being among the largest mosques in existence today.

Step 3:

Explore the bustling Medina of Casablanca and treat yourself to some shopping in the area's souks.

Step 4:

If you have time, you should go to the Corniche, which is a stunning beachfront promenade.

Step 5:

Then you should leave Casablanca for your next trip.

A 7-DAY TRAVEL SCHEDULE

DAY 1: MARRAKECH

What to Do:

1. Make your way to Marrakech, a bustling city known for the historic buildings and souks it contains.
2. Take some time to appreciate the stunning grounds and ornate architecture of the Bahia Palace.
3. Take a stroll through the lively Jemaa el-Fnaa square to take in the lively atmosphere created by the musicians, food merchants, and snake charmers who can be found there.
4. Wander through the lively souks and stop in some of the stores selling traditional souvenirs, spices, and crafts.
5. Have a traditional Moroccan lunch at one of the restaurants in the area.

DAY 2: MARRAKECH

What to Do:

1. Pay a visit to the well-known Koutoubia Mosque, which is also the largest mosque in Marrakech.
2. Pay a visit to the intriguing Berber Museum as well as the Majorelle Garden, which is famous for the lush vegetation it contains.
3. For an authentic spa experience, unwind and relax in a traditional hammam (also known as Moroccan baths).
4. The Saadian Tombs were built in the 16th century and are considered to be architectural masterpieces.
5. In the evening, head to a riad in your area for a delicious meal and some live entertainment.

DAY 3: ATLAS MOUNTAINS

What to Do:

1. Spend a day in the Atlas Mountains, which are conveniently located near Marrakech.
2. Pay a visit to the quaint village of Imlil and take a stroll through the jaw-dropping mountain landscape while on a guided tour.
3. Learn about the local culture by touring the traditional Berber communities.
4. Have lunch in a quaint town while enjoying a typical Berber meal.
5. Spend the night in a traditional Berber tent. After the sun has set, make your way back to Marrakech.

DAY 4: FES

What to Do:

1. Explore one of Morocco's oldest and most fascinating cities, Fes. Fes, with its UNESCO-listed Medina, has a perplexing maze of narrow alleyways and bustling markets.
2. Visit the venerable Al-Qarawiyyin Mosque, which is one of the oldest institutions of higher learning that is still in operation.
3. Enjoy a delicious meal at a nearby restaurant.
4. Visit the tanneries in Fes to see how leather is made the old-fashioned way.
5. Visit the Bou Inania Madrasa, which is a masterwork of architecture with beautiful tilework and detailed sculptures.

DAY 5: CHEFCHAOUEN

What to Do:

1. Situated in the Rif Mountains, Chefchaouen is also referred to as the "Blue City," and you will spend the day exploring this mountain town.
2. While you take a stroll through the winding, blue-washed streets, be sure to examine the charming architecture.
3. Travel to the square of Outa el Hammam and enjoy a cup of Moroccan mint tea at one of the local cafés.
4. Learn about the history and culture of the region by going to the Kasbah Museum.
5. In the evening, make your way back to Fes.
6. From the Spanish Mosque, take in the city's expansive perspectives.

DAY 6: CASABLANCA AND RABAT

What to Do:

1. Plan a trip to Casablanca, which is both the nation's capital and its largest city.
2. A trip to the magnificent Hassan II Mosque, which is one of the largest mosques in the world, is something that is highly recommended.
3. Take in the bustling atmosphere of the Corniche while you take a stroll along the water's edge.
4. Travel to Rabat, the capital city of Morocco.
5. While there, stop by the UNESCO World Heritage Site known as the Kasbah of the Udayas and take in the beautiful views of the Atlantic Ocean.
6. Visit the Hassan Tower and the Mohammed V Mausoleum while you're in the neighborhood.
7. Then head back to Casablanca for dinner and somewhere to spend the night.

DAY 7: ESSAOUIRA

What to Do:

1. Spend the day in the charming coastal town of Essaouira, which is well-known for its lovely beaches and buildings in the Portuguese style.
2. Explore the medina's winding lanes, which are filled with boutique stores and art galleries.
3. Visit the Skala de la Ville, a defensive sea wall that offers sweeping ocean vistas.
4. Indulge in fresh seafood at a neighborhood restaurant that overlooks the charming port.
5. Take a stroll along the promenade or relax on the beach.
6. At a later time, make your way back to Casablanca.

TRAVEL PLANS FOR THE WEEKEND

DAY 1:

Step 1:

Upon arrival in Marrakech, check into the accommodations that you have reserved.

Step 2:

Spend some time exploring the UNESCO World Heritage site, which is the lively medina. Pay a visit to the Koutoubia Mosque, the Bahia Palace, and the Saadian Tombs.

Step 3:

In the vicinity of the plaza Djemaa el-Fna, there is a restaurant where you can enjoy a traditional Moroccan meal while taking in the lively atmosphere of the area.

DAY 2:

Step 1:

Participate in a guided tour, or look into hiring a local guide.

Step 2:

Take a trip to the picturesque Imlil town, which can be found tucked away in the High Atlas Mountains.

Step 3:

Take a mule ride or go on a beautiful hike to discover the breathtaking landscapes and take in the incredible sights that are available.

Step 4:

Develop relationships with members of the local Berber populations to get knowledge of their culture and way of life.

Step 5:

When the day is done, head back to Marrakech and spend the evening relaxing on a rooftop patio with a glass of Moroccan mint tea.

DAY 3:

Step 1:

The Majorelle Garden is a stunning paradise of exotic flora and vibrant blue architecture, and it is recommended that you visit it in the morning.

Step 2:

Spend some time exploring the amazing museums that Marrakech has to offer, such as the Museum of Marrakech and the Berber Museum.

Step 3:

If you're looking for traditional handicrafts, spices, or apparel, you should check out the lively souks.

Step 4:

On your final night in Morocco, treat yourself to a traditional meal and try some local specialties like couscous or tagine.

SECOND ALTERNATIVE: FES AND CHEFCHAOUEN

DAY 1:

Step 1:

When you first arrive in Fes, select a lodging option and make yourself at home.

Step 2:

You should begin your exploration of Fes by going to the UNESCO-listed Medina, which is the world's largest urban quarter that does not allow cars.

Step 3:

While there, you should go to ancient buildings such as the Chouara Tannery, Al-Qarawiyyin Mosque, and Bou Inania Madrasa.

Step 4:

You should also take in the bustling atmosphere of the twisting streets packed with shops and artisans.

Day 2:

Step 1:

Spend the day exploring the "Blue City" of Chefchaouen, also known as the city. Admire the picturesque buildings that have been painted blue and are hidden away in the Rif Mountains.

Step 2:

Take your time on a stroll while shooting images of the charming streets that are perfect for Instagram.

Step 3:

Make sure to stop at the Grand Mosque as well as the Kasbah Museum.

Step 4:

You may get a breathtaking view of the city from the top of the Spanish Mosque.

Step 5:

If you want to sample authentic Moroccan cuisine, you should go to a traditional Moroccan restaurant.

Day 3:

Step 1:

Upon your return to Fes, continue your sightseeing by visiting the remaining attractions, such as the Royal Palace and the Nejjarine Museum of Wood Arts and Crafts.

Step 2:

Spend some time in the colorful souks of Fes, which are famous for their leather goods, textiles, and pottery.

Step 3:

Pamper yourself with a visit to a traditional Moroccan hammam.

Step 4:

Conclude your trip with a traditional Moroccan farewell lunch.

TRAVEL PLANS FOR TWO WEEKS

DAYS 1 AND 2: A TRIP TO MARRAKECH

Step 1:

When you get to Marrakech, you should investigate the bustling Medina and the famous Jemaa el-Fnaa square there.

Step 2:

You should also go to the gorgeous Majorelle Garden and Bahia Palace.

Step 3:

You should look at the Koutoubia Mosque and the Saadian Tombs.

Step 4:

While in Morocco, have a traditional lunch and experience the vibrant nightlife.

DAY 3 AND 4: VISITING THE ATLAS MOUNTAINS AND THE SAHARA DESERT

Step 1:

Spend a day in the Atlas Mountains, traveling there and exploring the picturesque mountain village of Imlil.

Step 2:

Go trekking in the Atlas Mountains and take in the breathtaking scenery.

Step 3:

Spend the night in a typical Berber community to immerse yourself in the culture and enjoy the warm hospitality of the locals.

Step 4:

Plan a trip to the Sahara Desert that lasts for multiple days and includes activities such as camel trekking and stargazing.

DAY 5-7: GOING TO FES

Step 1:

While in Fes, take some time to see the UNESCO World Heritage Site that is the Medina of Fes.

Step 2:

Pay a visit to the world-famous Al-Qarawiyyin Mosque, also known as the oldest university in the world.

Step 3:

Explore the historic Madrasas of Attarine and Bou Inania.

Step 4:

Find out more about the beautiful tanneries and bustling souks of Fes.

DAY 8 AND 9: ARRIVING CHEFCHAOUEN

Step 1:

Go to Chefchaouen, well known as the blue city.

Step 2:

Wander along the winding roads and take in the striking blue-painted buildings as you do so.

Step 3:

Make sure to stop at the Grand Mosque as well as the Kasbah Museum.

Step 4:

Hike up one of the surrounding mountains to get a magnificent view of the city.

DAY 10-12: VISITING ESSAOUIRA

Step 1:

Pay a visit to the charming coastal town of Essaouira.

Step 2:

Take in the sights of the historic Skala de la Ville and the Medina.

Step 3:

Relax and unwind on the breathtaking beaches by participating in water sports such as windsurfing or kitesurfing.

Step 4:

Savor freshly caught fish at one of the neighborhood eateries.

Step 5:

Take a boat ride across to the neighboring Mogador Island and explore it.

DAYS 13 AND 14: VISITING CASABLANCA AND RABAT

Step 1:

Explore one of the largest mosques in the world, the Hassan II Mosque, located in Casablanca.

Step 2:

Explore the modern heart of the city and the lively Corniche.

Step 3:

You can go to Rabat, the Moroccan capital, by rail.

Step 4:

Stop by some of the city's most famous landmarks, such as the Hassan Tower, the Royal Palace, and the Kasbah of the Udayas.

Step 5:

Experience the beauty of the coast as you wander along the Bouregreg River.

CHAPTER SIX
TOP ACCOMMODATION OPTIONS IN MOROCCO

The accommodations in Morocco are diverse, catering to a wide range of preferences, budgets, and requirements.

The following are some quite popular alternatives:

OPTION 1: RIADS

Riads are traditional mansions or castles in Morocco that have been renovated into luxurious lodgings. They typically have intricately tiled courtyards that are beautifully designed and a serene atmosphere throughout the building. Riads can be found in many Moroccan cities, including Marrakech, Fez, and Essaouira.

OPTION 2: LUXURIOUS HOTELS

Morocco is home to a good variety of high-end luxury hotels that offer first-rate amenities, first-rate service, and breathtaking décor. These hotels can be found in all of Morocco's major cities, including Marrakech, Casablanca, and Rabat.

OPTION 3: RESORTS

Along the coast and in popular tourist destinations, several resorts provide guests with a variety of recreational opportunities, including access to the beach, swimming pools, spa services, and other similar amenities. Beach resorts at Agadir, Essaouira, and Oualidia are among the most well-known in all of Morocco.

OPTION 4: GUESTHOUSES

Also known as "maisons d'hôtes," guesthouses provide a more personalized and secluded experience than hotels. They often are operated by families in the surrounding community and offer hospitable lodging, home-cooked meals, and opportunities to interact with the hosts. There are bed and breakfast establishments located all around the nation, including in rural areas.

OPTION 5: TRADITIONAL DESERT CAMPS

If you want to spend the night in the Sahara Desert, you can stay in one of the traditional desert camps. These camps offer a one-of-a-kind experience by enabling guests to partake in customary dining, spend the night in tents constructed in the style of those used by Bedouins, and take in the spectacular desert surroundings. Merzouga and Zagora are two famous destinations for campers interested in the desert.

OPTION 6: BUDGET HOTELS

Vacationers on a limited budget will find a variety of accommodations in Morocco that are within their price range. The facilities at these motels are rather basic, but the rooms are warm and inviting, and the rates are affordable. They can be discovered in the towns and cities located all around the country.

OPTION 7: ECO-LODGES

Morocco's rural areas and natural reserves are home to a variety of eco-lodges that cater to those who have a passion for nature and an awareness of the environment. In addition to providing visitors with the opportunity to take in the region's breathtaking scenery, these lodges place a strong emphasis on environmental responsibility.

NOTE: When choosing a hotel to stay in Morocco, it is important to think about the neighborhood, the available amenities and services, and the kind of experience you hope to have during your time there. This could include soaking up the local culture, lazing by the beach, or seeing ancient cities.

The following is a list of the ten best hotels in Morocco, which are located in various parts of the nation, along with a summary of the services and amenities that each one offers:

10 BEST HOTELS IN MOROCCO

1. Sofitel Essaouira Mogador Golf & Spa (Essaouira)

This hotel mixes contemporary convenience with the traditional allure of Morocco and is located close to the city of Essaouira on the seashore. It features luxurious guestrooms and suites, as well as a golf course, a spa, and many swimming pools. The hotel's beach club offers visitors not only direct access to a sandy beach but also the opportunity to engage in activities such as water sports and horseback riding.

2. The Mandarin Oriental, Marrakech (Marrakech)

This hotel, which is located in the heart of Marrakech and is surrounded by olive trees and verdant gardens, is a haven of peace. The hotel features a spa with traditional hammams, various restaurants, tennis facilities, and huge villas and suites with private pools. The guests can appreciate the peaceful ambiance as well as the impeccable service.

3. Royal Mansour Casablanca (Casablanca)

The Royal Mansour Casablanca is a luxurious hotel that can be found in the heart of Casablanca's business district. It provides guests with opulent rooms and suites decorated in a modern Moroccan style, as well as access to a spa, an outdoor pool, and breathtaking views of the city skyline. In addition, there are several upscale dining options and a bar at the hotel.

4. Palais Amani (Fez)

The Palais Amani is a typical Moroccan riad that has been converted into a boutique hotel. It can be found in the middle of the ancient city of Fez. A spa, a rooftop patio with panoramic views, and a Moroccan cookery school are some of the amenities that are available to guests. The Medina and all of its historical sites are open for guests to visit.

5. La Sultana Oualidia (Oualidia)

La Sultana is a boutique hotel that is well-known for its breathtaking views of the ocean and is located in the seaside town of Oualidia. It features opulent rooms and suites, as well as a spa, a heated pool, and direct access to a private beach. The guests can partake in activities such as birdwatching, water sports, and delectable seafood cuisine.

6. Selman Marrakech (Marrakech)

The Selman Marrakech, located in the city of Marrakech, is a luxurious hotel that was designed to resemble a palace and has exquisite Arabian horse stables. In addition to having a spa, many pools, and lush grounds, it has luxurious rooms and suites that each have a private patio. In addition, there are several options for upscale dining, a bar, and a cinema room inside the hotel.

7. The Royal Palm Tree Marrakech (Marrakech)

This magnificent resort is set on a vast estate close to Marrakech and offers big villas and suites with private pools and gardens. It is called Marrakech (Marrakech). In addition to a golf course, the resort features a kids' club, a spa, some different eating options, and more. Visitors have access to many amenities, including tennis courts, a fitness center, and a sizeable pool.

8. Kasbah Tamadot

Kasbah Tamadot is located in the Atlas Mountains. The magnificent resort known as Kasbah Tamadot, which is owned by Sir Richard Branson, can be found tucked away in the Atlas Mountains. The hotel features rooms and suites that are elegantly equipped, a spa, an infinity pool, and breathtaking views of the mountains in the background. Hiking, horseback riding, and visits to the neighboring Berber communities are some of the offered activities.

9. Marrakech La Mamounia

La Mamounia is a legendary hotel in Marrakech that mixes modern grandeur with the traditional elegance of Morocco. It has a wonderful interior design, a wide variety of dining options, and beautiful grounds. In addition to the excellent service and breathtaking vistas, guests can make use of the hotel's swimming pools, tennis courts, and fitness center during their stay.

10. The Royal Mansour Resort and Spa

The Marrakech is an amazing hotel located in the center of Marrakech that is famous for its excellent service. Each tourist is provided with their very own private riad, a typical

Moroccan house that comes fully stocked with amenities like rooftop patios, plunge pools, and butler service. The hotel provides guests with a wide variety of culinary options, as well as a spa and grounds that have been exquisitely planted.

CHAPTER SEVEN
FINEST RESTAURANTS AND CUISINE
EXPERIENCES IN MOROCCO

The diverse range of restaurants in Morocco, each showcasing the country's signature tastes and the meals that have been prepared traditionally for generations, results in a gastronomically satisfying experience.

Moroccan cuisine is well-known for its tasty ingredients, aromatic spices, and diverse spectrum of culinary influences that go into its preparation. By combining the flavors of traditional Berber, Arab, Moorish, and Mediterranean cuisines, it produces a gourmet experience that is both colorful and unique.

The following is a list of delicious Moroccan dishes that you really must try, along with some suggestions as to where you may get them:

TOP SAVORY DISHES IN MOROCCO

1. Tagine

Tagine is a classic dish from Morocco that is cooked in a clay pot shaped like a cone. Vegetables, an assortment of spices, and tender cuts of meat (such as chicken or lamb) are common components of this dish. Restaurants such as Le Foundouk in Marrakech and Restaurant Dar Hatim in Fes are known for the delectable tagines they feed their customers.

2. Couscous

Couscous is a dish made of steamed semolina grain that is served with a delectable stew of meat, vegetables, and occasionally dried fruits. Couscous is considered a staple diet in Morocco. Visit Restaurant Al Fassia in Marrakech or Restaurant Numero 7 in Casablanca if you are interested in tasting couscous that is prepared traditionally.

3. Pastilla

Pastilla is a kind of pie that combines salty and sweet flavors; it's made with seasoned almonds, shredded chicken or pigeon, and thin, crispy layers of dough. Experience some of the greatest pastillas in all of Morocco at the legendary La Mamounia Hotel in Marrakech.

4. Harira

Harira is a substantial and warm soup that is created with tomatoes, lentils, and chickpeas, and it is seasoned with a variety of delectable spices. It is commonly eaten as an appetizer or during the holy month of Ramadan. You can have some delicious harira at Café Clock in Fes or Café des Épices in Marrakech. Both of these restaurants are in Morocco.

5. Mechoui

Mechoui is a mouthwatering whole roasted leg of lamb or sheep that has been carefully prepared to bring forth its flavor. Mechoui is a dish that many people like eating on holidays and other special occasions. Restaurant Al Mounia in Casablanca and Restaurant Amal in Marrakech are also great places to try it.

6. Zaalouk

Zaalouk is a salad composed of eggplant, tomatoes, garlic, olive oil, and various spices; it has a smokey flavor and savory flavor. Bread is typically served alongside it to sop up the dip. Zaalouk is a wonderful dish that can be enjoyed in Marrakech at Café Arabe and in Chefchaouen at Café Clock.

7. Briouats

Briouats are savory pastries that can be baked or fried, and they can be packed with a variety of contents, such as cheese, minced meat, or shellfish. These can be delectable. Restaurant Tissemlal and Restaurant Aladdin both offer some delicious briouats, and you may try them out if you go to the old city of Chefchaouen.

8. Tanjia

Tanjia is a traditional dish from Marrakech in which the meat, most commonly beef, is braised in olive oil, herbs, and spices while also being seasoned with preserved lemon. You may get tanjia at the restaurant Dar Zellij or at one of the food carts that are located near the Djemaa el-Fna plaza in Marrakech.

9. Msemen

Msemen is a square pancake with a flaky texture that is made by folding dough and frying it until it is brown and crispy. Snacking on it or having it for breakfast are two common ways to consume it. Look for msemen at your neighborhood bakeries, such as the Patisserie des Princes in Marrakech or the Boulangerie de la Paix in Casablanca.

10. Mint Tea

This is a traditional beverage in Morocco. Mint tea is a vital component of the country's culture. Sugar, green tea leaves, and fresh mint leaves are the three primary ingredients in this beverage. Café Hafa in Tangier and La Maison Arabe in Marrakech are two Moroccan restaurants that serve mint tea in cold cups.

11. Rfissa

Rfissa is a comfortable dish that is produced by simmering shredded chicken, lentils, and thin layers of msemen, which is a sort of Moroccan pancake in a broth that is seasoned with various spices. It is a dish that is traditionally cooked for important events, such as weddings and other celebrations.

12. Chebakia

Chebakia is a pastry that resembles a flower and is sweet and crunchy on the outside. It is created with sesame seeds, honey, orange blossom water, and spices. During the holy month of Ramadan, people often eat chebakia, which may be purchased at local bakeries.

13. Jben

Jben is a mild and creamy white cheese that is traditionally accompanied by olives and bread. You may find Jben in the local markets and cheese shops. It is an item that is commonly used in Moroccan salads.

14. Khlea

Khlea is a traditional preserved meat dish that is prepared by slowly simmering beef or lamb with various spices such as cumin, garlic, and fenugreek. It is frequently found in traditional recipes and can be purchased in some stores that specialize in the sale of gourmet foods.

15. Seffa Medfouna

The sweet and savory dish known as "Seffa Medfouna" is prepared with steamed vermicelli noodles, chicken, almonds, and powdered sugar. It is a dish that is frequently served at weddings and other formal events.

16. Makfoul

Makfoul is a meal consisting of caramelized onions that have been slow-cooked with spices and are typically used as a side dish or condiment. You can get makfoul at a lot of the local eateries, and it goes well with a lot of other Moroccan foods.

17. Sardines à la Chermoula

Sardines à la Chermoula are sardines that have been grilled and then marinated in a flavorful sauce that is created with garlic, lemon, cilantro, and spices. Essaouira and other coastal communities like it have made it one of their most popular options for food sold on the street.

The following is a list of the ten best restaurants in Morocco, which can be found in different regions of the nation, along with information about the services and amenities that are available to tourists:

10 BEST RESTAURANTS IN MOROCCO

1. Al Fassia (Located in Marrakech)

Al Fassia is a restaurant in Marrakech that has been owned and operated by the same family for many years and serves traditional Moroccan food. The restaurant is well-known for its friendly service and genuine flavor profiles, and it provides an atmosphere that is cozy and intimate. Both residents and tourists frequent this restaurant because of its affordable prices and its emphasis on cooking traditionally.

2. Rick's Café (Located in Casablanca)

This establishment was inspired by the film "Casablanca," and it recreates the atmosphere of a piano bar from the 1940s. The restaurant offers a rooftop patio with panoramic views of the city, and the menu comprises a combination of Moroccan and international dishes as well as other cuisines from across the world. The experience is made more valuable by the presence of a nostalgic ambiance, even though the prices are greater.

3. Le Comptoir Darna (Located inMarrakech)

Located in Marrakech, Le Comptoir Darna is a restaurant that is noted for its colorful atmosphere and live entertainment. The restaurant frequently showcases belly dancing and live music acts, and the food features a fusion of Moroccan and foreign flavors and ingredients. The prices are reasonable, and both residents and tourists frequent this destination due to its popularity.

4. La Mamounia (Located in Marrakech)

This is a reputable luxury hotel in Marrakech, and it offers numerous options for upmarket dining. The restaurants within La Mamounia cater to a wide range of preferences, serving everything from traditional Moroccan cuisine to foreign specialties. Although the costs are more expensive, the exceptional service and luxurious surroundings offer an experience that is hard to forget.

5. Restaurant Tobsil (Located in Essaouira)

Tucked away in the beach town of Essaouira is a restaurant recognized for its superb Moroccan cuisine. Restaurant Tobsil is a hidden gem. The restaurant has a warm and inviting ambiance, complete with a fireplace and traditional seating, which contributes to the restaurant's overall allure. Since the prices are not exorbitant, tourists won't have any trouble affording it.

6. Dar Zellij (Located in Marrakech)

This restaurant, which is located in the Medina of Marrakech and is housed in a riad that has been renovated, provides a refined dining experience. The restaurant's food is focused on traditional Moroccan cuisine, and the gorgeous traditional decor complements the meal. Although the costs are a little bit higher than average, the value of the meal and the overall experience is well worth it.

7. La Sqala (Located in Casablanca)

La Sqala is a restaurant in Casablanca that is located close to the old medina of the city. It is built in a medieval stronghold that features a stunning garden patio. Tagines and couscous are only two of the typical Moroccan meals that can be found on the menu at this enchanting restaurant. The restaurant is well-known for its friendly service as well as its moderately priced meals.

8. Villa Josephine

Located in Tangier, Villa Josephine is a fine dining establishment that provides a sophisticated ambiance. This restaurant has a view of the Mediterranean Sea. The cuisine on the menu is a fusion of Moroccan and Mediterranean styles, with a primary focus on various types of fresh fish. Even if the costs are more expensive, the exceptional service and breathtaking vistas make it an experience that is hard to forget.

9. Cafe Clock (Located in Fes)

Located at the heart of the Medina of Fes, Cafe Clock is famous for its lively atmosphere as well as its mouthwatering cuisine. In addition to frequently hosting cultural events and live music performances, they specialize in serving fusion cuisine inspired by Moroccan street food. The costs are fair and can accommodate customers with a variety of financial constraints.

10. Le Jardin (Located in Marrakech)

This restaurant, which can be found in the center of Marrakech, is known for its exquisite dining options that are offered outside in a garden setting. The restaurant is known for its combination of Moroccan and world food, as well as its warm and welcoming service and laid-back ambiance. The prices are reasonable, making it possible for tourists to afford it.

CHAPTER EIGHT
VIBRANT NIGHTLIFE AND FESTIVITY IN MOROCCO

The nighttime scene in Morocco is both active and diversified, and it features a wide range of activities to accommodate a variety of tastes and geographic locations across the country.

The following is a view of the kinds of activities and nightlife that may be found in different regions of Morocco:

Nightlife in Marrakech

Marrakech is a city that is known for its lively atmosphere and has a booming nightlife scene. The city comes to life thanks to its many vibrant nightclubs, rooftop bars, and music venues. The well-known Jemaa el-Fnaa square is transformed into a hub of activity thanks to the presence of street performers, food stalls, and live music. You can also engage in traditional Moroccan entertainment, such as belly dancing and live music performances at several different sites throughout the country.

Nightlife in Casablanca

Casablanca is the largest city in Morocco as well as the country's capital. Additionally, it serves as the primary commercial hub of the nation. The neighborhoods of Ain Diab and Maarif, in particular, are home to a significant number of the city's most fashionable bars, clubs, and lounges. The beach clubs and waterfront restaurants in the Corniche's coastline district are well-known for the beautiful views that they offer while pouring cocktails to customers.

Nightlife in Essaouira

Essaouira is a laid-back and bohemian community that is located on the coast of Morocco. In the evenings, Essaouira's medina (the city's old town) comes alive with street performers, singers, and merchants selling regional wares along its twisting pathways. You have the option of taking in live music performances, exploring the vibrant night market, and dining at neighborhood eateries that serve fresh seafood.

Nightlife in Tangier

Tangier is renowned for its multiethnic atmosphere and rich artistic heritage, and it is also known for the unique nightlife experience it provides. The city boasts a thriving arts and music culture thanks to the large number of jazz clubs and other live music venues. There are many trendy bars and cafes in the area where you can experience a lively atmosphere. Some of these establishments can be found on the well-known Boulevard Pasteur and in the neighborhood around the Grand Socco.

Nightlife in Fes

The old medina of Fes, which is known for its extensive cultural past, comes to life during the evenings. You can take a stroll through the bustling streets of the medina, dine at restaurants serving traditional Moroccan cuisine, and see traditional musical performances. The Batha Square is a popular place to go to watch live entertainment because of its lively atmosphere.

Nightlife in Agadir

On the southwestern coast of Morocco, in the city of Agadir, you may have the opportunity to have a more relaxed evening. The city is well-known for its breathtaking coastline, which features a wide variety of beach clubs, pubs, and cafes for visitors to enjoy while they take in the view. Agadir also has a flourishing casino business, which is great news for anyone who enjoys trying their luck at the tables.

Nightlife in Chefchaouen

In comparison to other, larger towns, Chefchaouen is recognized for having a more laid-back nightlife with breathtaking views of the surrounding mountains. You can have a relaxing evening by wandering about the enticing blue medina, making stops at rooftop cafes, and indulging in local cuisine. In the well-known meeting spot known as Plaza Uta el-Hammam, you will have the opportunity to relax and take in the ambiance.

REMEMBER: In addition to its vibrant nightlife, Morocco provides visitors with a diverse selection of daytime activities, such as touring historical sites, hiking in the Atlas Mountains, riding camels through the Sahara Desert, going to traditional Moroccan hammams, shopping in vibrant souks, and indulging in mouthwatering Moroccan cuisine. The fact that different regions of the country each have their unique attractions and things to do ensures that travelers will have a range of experiences that are unique and engaging.

FESTIVE CELEBRATIONS IN MOROCCO

Morocco is well-known for having a wide range of vibrant and thrilling annual cultural festivals throughout the country.

People living in the country, as well as visitors to the country, enjoy taking part in the festivities of these festivals, which serve to shed light on the nation's illustrious history and customs. The following is a list of 20 well-known Moroccan festivals, including the dates of the festivals, the events that are linked with them, and the activities that can be enjoyed by both Moroccans and tourists:

1. Ramadan (The date changes every year)

Muslims all around the world, including those in Morocco, observe the holy month of Ramadan, which is considered to be one of the most important holidays in the Islamic calendar.

From the time the sun rises until it sets, the locals observe a fast during which they pray and consume special meals known as iftar.

Tourists may take part in the joyful atmosphere, indulge in traditional Moroccan desserts, and marvel at the wonderfully decorated mosques and streets in Morocco.

2. Eid al-Fitr (The date changes every year)

This holiday, which marks the end of the month-long fasting period known as Ramadan, is commemorated with joyous celebrations.

Residents of the area participate in activities like giving alms, attending mosque prayers, and exchanging gifts.

Guests have the opportunity to take part in neighborhood events, try traditional Eid fare, and soak up the celebratory atmosphere.

3. Gnaoua World Music Festival (Held in June)

This event, which is hosted in Essaouira, is held to honor traditional Gnaoua music, which is a combination of Berber, Arab, and African sounds.

Gnaoua music is played by regional and international musicians, attracting music fans from all over the world.

Workshops, live music performances, and Essaouira's buzzing atmosphere are all available for tourists to experience while they are in town.

4. Fes Festival of World Sacred Music (Held in June)

This Fes event encourages intercultural communication through performances of religious music.

Different styles of spiritual music are performed by regional and international musicians.

Visitors have the opportunity to explore the old city of Fes while also attending concerts, workshops, and conferences.

5. The Marrakech Popular Arts Festival (Held in July)

The city of Marrakech is the location of this exciting event, which highlights the traditional arts and crafts of Morocco.

Marrakech is a city in Morocco that is known for its vivid parades, artistic displays, and lively environment.

Visitors may see locals put on public performances on the streets, including music, dance, and telling stories.

6. Eid al-Adha (The date changes every year)

Eid al-Adha, commonly known as the "Festival of Sacrifice," is a holiday that celebrates Ibrahim's willingness to offer his son as a sacrifice.

The locals pray, sacrifice animals, and share meat with their loved ones, friends, and others who are less fortunate to show their gratitude.

Guests will get the opportunity to engage in communal meals, enjoy the warmth and hospitality of Moroccan families, and watch traditional rites.

7. Imilchil Marriage Festival (Held in September)

This unique event is conducted in the village of Imilchil and recognizes all of the Berber couples in the area who tied the knot at the same time.

Matchmaking events are held in the community, during which participants dress in traditional clothing and engage in activities such as singing and dancing.

Visitors have the opportunity to experience local traditions first-hand, observe music and dance performances, and travel through the High Atlas Mountains, which are known for their stunning scenery.

8. Erfoud Date Festival (Held in October)

This festival, which takes place in Erfoud, is held in commemoration of the abundant date crop in the surrounding area.

Residents of the area compete in cooking contests and date-picking tournaments and put on traditional performances of music and dancing.

Guests will have the opportunity to try a variety of dates, see camel races, and learn about the production and processing of dates.

9. International Nomads Festival (Held in November)

This celebration, which honors the nomadic way of life of the people who live in the Sahara Desert, takes place in M'Hamid El Ghizlane.

During this event, camels are raced, poems are read, traditional music is performed, and locals display their handicrafts.

Guests will have the opportunity to ride camels, experience life in the desert, listen to captivating stories, and view stunning sunsets.

10. Timitar Festival (Held in July)

This festival celebrates the Amazigh (Berber) way of life and music in Agadir.

Regional and international performers perform traditional Amazigh music as well as jazz and fusion styles of music.

While in Agadir, tourists may take in live performances, get their groove on to pulsating rhythms, and take pleasant walks along the city's magnificent coastline.

11. Rose Festival (Held in May)

This festival is held in the town of Kelaat M'gouna and honors the rose blooming in the Dades Valley.

Locals organize parades, beauty contests, and concerts, all of which are complemented by the lovely aroma of roses.

Visitors will be able to participate in cultural events, purchase items produced from roses, and see the harvesting of roses.

12. Essaouira Gnaoua and World Music Festival (Held in June)

This festival celebrates the rose blooming in the Dades Valley and takes place in the town of Kelaat M'gouna.

The enticing scent of roses wafts through the air during the parades, beauty pageants, and concerts that the community puts on.

Visitors will be able to participate in cultural events, purchase items produced from roses, and see the harvesting of roses.

13. The National Cherry Festival (Held in June)

This takes place in June and celebrates the harvest of cherries. This event is conducted in Sefrou.

Cherry-picking competitions, parades, and folklore performances are some of the events that are organized by the residents.

Guests can indulge in some mouthwatering cherries, take a stroll through the picturesque village, and witness some age-old customs.

14. Tan-Tan Moussem (Held in November)

The Tan-Tan Moussem is an annual gathering of Saharan tribes that takes place in Tan-Tan.

During this event, the people celebrate their rich cultural history by racing camels, displaying horses, performing music and dancing, and listening to traditional songs.

Guests have the opportunity to take part in entertaining performances, gain insight into Saharan traditions, and experience a taste of nomadic life.

15. Marrakech International Film Festival (Held in November/December)

This renowned film festival brings together films from around the world with those produced in the city of Marrakech.

The festival recognizes cinematic achievements, hosts activities on the red carpet, and screens a selection of films.

Tourists have the opportunity to attend movie screenings, meet influential businesspeople, and see Marrakech.

16. Asilah Arts Festival (Held in August)

This festival, which is held in the city of Asilah, which is located on the seashore, emphasizes cross-cultural interaction, music, and visual arts.

Artists from all over the world, both local and international, are responsible for painting murals. These artists also perform dance and music.

Concerts, vibrant art exhibits, and the laid-back vibe of the beach are all available for guests to enjoy during their time in Asilah.

17. Tafraoute Almond Blossom Festival (Held in February)

This festival, held in Tafraoute, pays tribute to the blossoming almond trees that may be seen in the Anti-Atlas region.

Handicraft fairs, poetry readings, traditional music performances, and parades are all organized and hosted by locals.

Guests will get the opportunity to admire the beautiful almond blossoms, indulge in regional cuisine that features almonds, and discover the surrounding landscape.

18. Festival of Fantasia (Held in July/August)

Throughout the entire country of Morocco, the traditional equestrian competition known as Fantasia is celebrated.

Locals dressed in traditional garb perform equestrian acrobatics while firing blank rounds from guns loaded with gunpowder.

Visitors can enjoy entertaining horse exhibitions, demonstrations of Moroccan horsemanship, and cultural exhibits during their stay.

19. Sahara Festival (November)

This festival, which takes place in Rissani, showcases the many cultural practices of the Sahara Desert.

Camels are raced, poetry is read, traditional music is performed, and nomadic sports are played by the people during this festival, which takes place in Rissani in November.

Guests will get the opportunity to observe mesmerizing desert performances, ride camels, investigate native handicrafts, and even live in the desert.

20. Mawazine World Rhythms Festival (Held in June)

Renowned musicians from all over the world congregate in Rabat for this prestigious music festival, which takes place every year in the city.

There are live performances of a wide variety of musical genres, including pop, rock, hip-hop, and traditional Moroccan music.

Also featured are performances of traditional Moroccan music. There are a variety of musical traditions that may be experienced, as well as the capital city of Rabat, which can be explored and also hosts performances.

All of these festivals offer both locals and visitors the chance to participate in the commemoration of traditional practices, observe musical and dance performances, enjoy mouthwatering cuisine, and gain a comprehensive understanding of the vibrant culture of this fascinating country. In addition to this, they offer a glimpse into the illustrious cultural history of Morocco.

CHAPTER NINE
EXPLORING MOROCCAN SHOPPING AND SOUVENIR

Tourists can choose from several different retail complexes in Morocco that are designed to meet their requirements and interests.

The following is a list of some of the most well-known shopping centers located in several Moroccan cities, along with the categories of items that may be purchased at these centers:

TOP SHOPPING PLACES IN MOROCCO

1. Morocco Mall (Located in Casablanca)

The Morocco Mall, which can be found in Casablanca, is one of the largest shopping centers in all of Africa. A vast variety of local and international brands, upscale boutiques, and a wide range of dining options can be found there. You can find a variety of items here, including trendy apparel and accessories, cosmetics, gadgets, and even home decor. In addition, the shopping center features an extensive indoor amusement park, a movie theater, and an aquarium.

2. Menara Mall (Located in Marrakech)

Menara Mall, which is located in Marrakech, provides a shopping experience that is unlike any other. It features modern design elements alongside traditional Moroccan architecture, which is on display there. The shopping center is home to a diverse selection of stores providing a range of goods, including clothing, handicrafts, spices, and other regional specialties. Traditional Moroccan handicrafts such as carpets, ceramics, leather goods, and jewelry are also available for purchase here.

3. Almazar Mall (Located in Rabat)

Almazar Mall, which is located in Rabat, offers a variety of retail opportunities in one location. It offers a variety of dining alternatives, as well as a hypermarket, fashion stores, electronic outlet stores, beauty and wellness facilities, and retail outlets. The shopping center also features a variety of leisure venues, such as a movie complex and a play area for children.

4. Tanger City Mall (Located in Tangier)

Located in Tangier, the Tanger City Mall is a popular location for shoppers. It is home to a wide range of shops selling a variety of products, including fashion garments and accessories, cosmetics, household items, electronics, and more. In addition, the shopping center is home to many restaurants, a grocery, and a multiplex cinema. Its proximity to the heart of the city and user-friendliness make it an attractive destination for vacationers.

5. Marina Shopping Center (Located in Agadir)

This lively shopping destination can be found in the city of Agadir, which is located on the coast. It offers a variety of brands, including apparel, athletics, footwear, and accessories, from both local and international manufacturers. With its waterfront location, restaurants, and cafes, as well as its breathtaking panorama of the marina, the shopping center makes for an enjoyable experience overall.

6. Anfaplace Shopping Center (Located in Casablanca)

Located in Casablanca, the Anfaplace Shopping Center is well-known for its contemporary architecture as well as its beachside setting. It is home to a wide range of stores providing a variety of goods, including clothes, accessories, cosmetics, and electrical goods. In addition, the shopping center features some different dining establishments, as well as cafes and a multiplex theater. It is a well-known destination for people looking to shop as well as relax.

NOTE: It is important to bring to your notice that in addition to these few instances, there are a great number of different shopping centers located all around the country of Morocco. Neighborhood markets known as "souks" are also common in Moroccan cities and towns. These markets offer a vibrant and authentic shopping experience with a variety of traditional goods such as fabrics, spices, pottery, and handicrafts. Exploring these marketplaces is a great way to both find one-of-a-kind things and get a feel for the culture of the area.

SOUVENIRS IN MOROCCO

Morocco is well-known for its lively markets, which are referred to as souks, and within these markets, you may find a wide variety of one-of-a-kind souvenirs.

The following is a list of popular Moroccan souvenirs, along with locations where they can be purchased:

1. Moroccan Carpets

Moroccan carpets are stunning rugs that are hand-woven and include a broad variety of designs and color combinations. They are common in Marrakech, Fes, and Chefchaouen, among other cities in Morocco. The best place to look for them is in the Medina, which is where the souks are located, and there you can also visit stores that specialize in carpets.

2. Leather Goods

Morocco is well-known for its leather goods, which include footwear, outerwear, and handbags, among other things. Tanneries in well-known Moroccan locations such as Fes and Marrakech are the places where traditional leather goods are created. Visit the Chouara Tannery leather bazaar in Fes or the Leather Souk in Marrakech to get a wide selection of leather goods. Both of these markets are located in Morocco.

3. Moroccan Pottery

Traditional Moroccan pottery makes beautiful tagines, plates, and bowls, all of which are excellent gift options. It is common knowledge that Safi is famous for its ceramics; hence, if you are in search of unique goods, you should look at the area's workshops and shops. The area of Marrakech that is located close to Bab El Khemis and the Dar Bellarj Foundation is well-known for its pottery.

4. Moroccan Spices

The aromatic spices of Morocco are an excellent present to take back with you to your native country. Spice markets, also known as "souks des épices," are located in cities like Marrakech and Fes in Morocco. These shops stock a wide range of spices, some of which include cumin, saffron, cinnamon, and Ras el Hanout. These marketplaces are often located within the bustling medinas of their respective cities.

5. Traditional Moroccan Clothing

Traditional Moroccan clothing may be purchased at markets all around the country. This includes babouches, which are leather shoes, and djellabas, which are long robes. In Marrakech, the Souk Cherratine and the Souk Semmarine are two fantastic markets to visit if you are interested in purchasing new clothing or footwear.

6. Moroccan Lanterns

Intricately built lanterns made of metal or colored glass are a popular choice for a gift to bring home from Morocco. In Marrakech, particularly in Medina, one may find an abundance of lanterns in a wide variety of styles and colors. The Souk El Had is well known for its magnificent selection of Moroccan lamps, which are available for purchase there.

7. Berber Craft

One type of gift that is truly one of a kind is a Berber craft. These handicrafts reflect the rich cultural heritage of the local Berber population. These handicrafts include items carved out of wood, jewelry made out of silver, and textiles woven together. The High Atlas Mountains and cities such as Chefchaouen and Essaouira are two places in Morocco where you may find an abundance of Berber crafts.

8. Argan Oil

The argan tree is the source of the natural oil that is used in the manufacture of cosmetics and products for the care of hair and skin. It can be purchased in Essaouira and Marrakech at shops that specialize in the item.

9. Moroccan Musical Instruments

Exceptional souvenirs encompass musical instruments such as the oud (a stringed instrument) and darbuka (a hand drum). Explore the musical instrument shops in Essaouira or Marrakech to find these treasures."

10. Moroccan Dates

Dates from Morocco Dates from Morocco are well-known for their delicious flavor. They are sold in local grocery stores and specialty shops all across the country.

11. Moroccan Argan Wood Products

Essaouira's specialty shops sell a variety of handcrafted products made from argan wood, including bowls, chopping boards, and other kitchenware.

12. Traditional Moroccan Handicrafts

The Medinas are home to a wide array of traditional Moroccan handicrafts, including ceramics, metalwork, and woodwork. These items can be found quite easily in Marrakech and Fes, two of Morocco's most famous cities.

13. Moroccan Sweets

Indulge in some baklava, gazelle horns, and almond candies from Morocco for a sweet reward for yourself. These can be found at local bakeries and confectionery stores all around the country of Morocco.

CONCLUSION

This book, *'Morocco Travel Guide,'* has served as your trusted companion on this journey of exploration through Morocco's rich landscapes, cultural gems, and vibrant experiences. From understanding what essentials you need to embark on a Moroccan adventure to discover the many benefits of such a voyage, we've covered the foundations of an unforgettable trip. You've also been introduced to the captivating places that await tourists in Morocco, ranging from ancient cities to breathtaking natural wonders.

As we delved into the heart of adventure, you were equipped with a wealth of outdoor activities to relish and practical travel plans to make your journey seamless. We explored top accommodation choices, ensuring you rest in comfort during your travels, and unveiled the finest restaurants and Moroccan cuisine to delight your taste buds. When the sun sets, Morocco's nightlife and festivities come alive, making your evenings as memorable as your days.

Finally, we navigated the maze of Moroccan shopping, revealing the unique souvenirs and treasures to take home.

So, as you conclude this journey through the pages of this book, may you find yourself not just a traveler but an explorer, not merely a tourist but a seeker of the unique. Morocco's allure lies in its ability to embrace you, body and soul, and leave an indelible mark.

Whether you're captivated by its history, enamored by its landscapes, or enchanted by its culture, Morocco has a place for you. As you step out into the world, ready to embark on your Moroccan adventure, may your voyage be filled with wonder, joy, and unforgettable memories. Enjoy your trip!

Printed in Great Britain
by Amazon